At Issue

Environmental Racism and Classism

Other Books in the At Issue Series:

At Issue

Environmental Racism and Classism

Anne Cunningham, Book Editor

GREENHAVEN
PUBLISHING

Published in 2017 by Greenhaven Publishing, LLC
353 3rd Avenue, Suite 255, New York, NY 10010

Articles in Greenhaven Publishing anthologies are often edited for length to meet page
requirements. In addition, original titles of these works are changed to clearly present
the main thesis and to explicitly indicate the author's opinion. Every effort is made to
ensure that Greenhaven Publishing accurately reflects the original intent of the authors.
Every effort has been made to trace the owners of the copyrighted material.

Cover image: Lightspring/Shutterstock.com

Library of Congress Cataloging-in-Publication Data

Names: Cunningham, Anne.
Title: Environmental racism and classism / Anne Cunningham.
Description: New York : Greenhaven Publishing, 2017. | Series: At issue | Includes index.
Identifiers: LCCN ISBN 9781534500402 (pbk.) | ISBN 9781534500167 (library bound)
Subjects: LCSH: Environmental policy—United States. |
Racism — United States. | Classism—United States.
Classification: LCC GE180.C75 2017 | DDC 363.7'0560973—dc23

Manufactured in the United States of America

Website: http://greenhavenpublishing.com

Contents

Introduction

When we think of environmentalism, our first thoughts may go to issues of conservation such as how to save the Amazon rainforests or protect an endangered species of marine wildlife. However, a growing contingent of environmental activists are increasingly concerned with the many hazards and threats to a good quality of life and positive health in humanity's natural habitats— the rural, suburban, and urban dwellings and communities where ordinary people live, work, and play. The broad movement for environmental justice seeks acknowledgment and redress of the unequal distribution of environmental hazards and risks according to social factors such as economic class, social status, and race.

Within the movement for environmental justice, a compelling subset of thinkers and activists hold that race is the paramount issue affecting environmental justice. Indeed, to some, the very term "environmental justice" is problematic in that it downplays the ways in which racism functions as the central cause of environmental injustice. Beginning with a study by the Congressional General Accounting Office (GAO) in 1983, the reality of environmental racism has gradually gained traction. Since then, many more research studies have cited strong evidence that the people who live closest to dangerous sources of pollution are overwhelmingly people of color. In other words, there is a greater chance that a so-called LULU (Locally Unwanted Land Use) would be sited for a middle-income African-American community than it would for an even much lower income but still majority white area. According to the GAO study, in eight southeastern states, only twenty-five percent of toxic waste landfill sites were located in primarily white neighborhoods. Subsequent reports such as the landmark *Toxic Wastes and Race in the United States* published by the United Church of Christ's Commission for Racial Justice (CRJ) in 1987 provided much corroborating evidence underscoring the centrality of race for tough questions of environmental justice.

Robert Bullard, a leading opponent of environmental racism whose writing appears as a viewpoint in this resource, defines the issue of environmental racism as "any environmental policy, practice, or directive that differentially affects or disadvantages (whether intended or unintended) individuals, groups, or communities based on race or color" (Bullard 1993a). The key words above are "intended or unintended." Thus, an institution or governmental body need not have explicitly nefarious white-supremacist intentions to enact policy that is inherently racist. To begin with, minority groups usually have less political power, a problem exacerbated by board meetings that are often held at inconvenient locations or times, or conducted exclusively in English. These impediments to "procedural equity" can reduce a minority community's participation in decision-making, and ultimately erode self-determination. Moreover, a racist history of land-use policies has sometimes codified discriminatory practice as zoning law. In the case of residents of the primarily African-American Eno Road neighborhood in rural Tennessee, zoning ordinance allowed a waste site to poison their drinking water, but left nearby rural white communities' water unaffected. A recent court settlement for the many victims of illnesses caused by such blatant environmental racism is an important first step to rectify the abuse, and reiterate the existence of the problem.

Nonetheless, some authors from whom we will hear below claim that there is no such thing as environmental racism as such. Their viewpoints do not necessarily deny the reality of institutional racism, or environmental ills. Rather, their claim is that in a country where most of us have clean drinking water and basic health safeguards, environmental racism is a relatively minor issue, and simply an outgrowth of larger racial inequities in other systems such as education, employment, and housing, to take a few examples. Does the focus on environmental policy divert some governmental energy and resources away from these other issues? Undoubtedly. However, the denial of environmental racism outright may work as a rhetorical erasure, undermining how the struggle against environmental racism intersects with other anti-racist and classist projects.

Environmental racism is not just an American problem. European colonialism has long since exploited the resources of the Global South such as Africa, South America, and the Middle East, a process that continues today on a corporate level. The pursuit of profit is at the expense of local people, who find their living environments transformed into a wasteland of pollution and social chaos once all the valuable materials have been extracted. Moreover, the movement for climate justice points out that many nations that burn the least carbon are bearing the considerable costs of devastating weather events, sea level rise caused by dangerous levels of CO_2 in the atmosphere caused by wealthier, heavily industrialized nations. International summits addressing climate change are taking these factors into account thanks to the efforts of this movement.

The viewpoints that follow each approach environmental injustice from overlapping angles. While their conclusions differ, taken together they demonstrate that much must still be done to ensure that all people have access to the basics of a healthy life, regardless of race, class, and geography.

1

Building Momentum for the Environmental Justice Movement

Renee Skelton and Vernice Miller

Renee Skelton is an author and activist, and Vernice Miller-Travis cofounded WE ACT for Environmental Justice, a community based organization in New York City.

The Environmental Justice Movement began in the 1960s, later coalescing around a series of protests against a PCB dumping site in North Carolina. Since then, several studies have proven that neighborhoods with a high concentration of people of color are disproportionately sited for unwanted toxic projects such as waste dumps. In 1994, President Bill Clinton signed an Executive Order directing federal agencies to address the adverse health effects of policies on low-income people and people of color. The environmental justice movement has since continued to build strength.

Environmental justice is an important part of the struggle to improve and maintain a clean and healthful environment, especially for those who have traditionally lived, worked, and played closest to the sources of pollution.

Championed primarily by African-Americans, Latinos, Asians and Pacific Islanders, and Native Americans, the environmental justice movement addresses a statistical fact: people who live, work,

"The Environmental Justice Movement," Renee Skelton and Vernice Miller, Natural Resources Defense Council, March 17, 2016. https://www.nrdc.org/stories/environmental-justice-movement. Reprinted with permission from the Natural Resources Defense Council.

and play in America's most polluted environments are commonl[ ]people of color and the poor. Environmental justice advocates have shown that this is no accident. Communities of color, which are often poor, are routinely targeted to host facilities that have negative environmental impacts—say, a landfill, dirty industrial plant or truck depot. The statistics provide clear evidence of what the movement rightly calls "environmental racism." Communities of color have been battling this injustice for decades.

A Movement Sparks

Poor, rural, and overwhelmingly black, Warren County, North Carolina, might seem an unlikely spot for the birth of a political movement. But when the state government decided that the county would make a perfect home for 6,000 truckloads of soil laced with toxic PCBs, the county became the focus of national attention.

The dump trucks first rolled into Warren County in mid-September, 1982, headed for a newly constructed hazardous waste landfill in the small community of Afton. But many frustrated residents and their allies, furious that state officials had dismissed concerns over PCBs leaching into drinking water supplies, met the trucks. And they stopped them, lying down on roads leading into the landfill. Six weeks of marches and nonviolent street protests followed, and more than 500 people were arrested—the first arrests in U.S. history over the siting of a landfill.

The people of Warren County ultimately lost the battle; the toxic waste was eventually deposited in that landfill. But their story—one of ordinary people driven to desperate measures to protect their homes from a toxic assault—drew national media attention and fired the imagination of people across the country who had lived through similar injustice. The street protests and legal challenges mounted by the people of Warren County to fight the landfill are considered by many to be the first major milestone in the national movement for environmental justice.

Other communities of color had organized to oppose environmental threats before Warren County. In the early 1960s,

Latino farm workers organized by Cesar Chavez fought for workplace rights, including protection from harmful pesticides in the farm fields of California's San Joaquin valley. In 1967, African-American students took to the streets of Houston to oppose a city garbage dump in their community that had claimed the lives of two children. In 1968, residents of West Harlem, in New York City, fought unsuccessfully against the siting of a sewage treatment plant in their community. But the Warren County protests marked the first instance of an environmental protest by people of color that garnered widespread national attention.

The Facts of Environmental Racism

To civil rights activists looking on as the events in Warren County played out, the actions of the North Carolina state government in forcing a toxic landfill onto a small African-American community were an extension of the racism they had encountered for decades in housing, education, and employment. But this time, it was *environmental* racism.

The Afton protests energized a new faction within the civil rights movement that saw the environment as another front in the struggle for justice. Many early environmental justice leaders came out of the civil rights movement. They brought to the environmental movement the same tactics they had used in civil rights struggles—marches, petitions, rallies, coalition building, community empowerment through education, litigation and nonviolent direct action. Many veterans of the civil rights movement—often affiliated with black churches — showed up in Afton, helping to attract national media attention. Among them were Reverend Ben Chavis and Reverend Joseph Lowery, then of the Southern Christian Leadership Conference, and Reverend Leon White of the United Church of Christ's Commission for Racial Justice.

In the wake of the Afton protests, environmental justice activists looked around the nation and saw a pattern: Pollution-producing facilities are often sited in poor communities of color.

No one wants a factory, a landfill or a diesel bus garage for a neighbor. But corporate decision makers, regulatory agencies, and local planning and zoning boards had learned that it was easier to site such facilities in low-income African-American or Latino communities than in primarily white, middle-to-upper-income communities. Poor communities and communities of color usually lacked connections to decision makers on zoning boards or city councils that could protect their interests. Often they could not afford to hire the technical and legal expertise they'd need to fight a siting. They often lacked access to information about how their new "neighbor's" pollution would affect people's health. And in the case of Latino communities, important information in English-only documents was out of reach for affected residents who spoke only Spanish.

Several studies published in the 1980s and early 1990s gave charges of environmental racism new credibility. Walter Fauntroy, District of Columbia Congressional Delegate and then-chair of the Congressional Black Caucus, took part in the Afton protests. When Fauntroy returned to Washington, he tasked Congress's General Accounting Office with determining whether communities of color suffered disproportionate negative impacts from the siting and construction of hazardous waste landfills within them. The GAO study was published in 1983, and revealed that three-quarters of the hazardous waste landfill sites in eight southeastern states were located in primarily poor, African-American, and Latino communities.

More evidence of environmental racism came through the efforts of the United Church of Christ's Commission for Racial Justice (CRJ), under the leadership of Reverend Benjamin Chavis, who had also stood with the protesters at Afton. With Chavis serving as its director, the CRJ published *Toxic Wastes and Race in the United States*, a 1987 report that became an indispensable tool in galvanizing support for environmental justice action. The report, by the UCC's Director of Research Charles Lee, showed that race was the single most important factor in determining where toxic waste facilities were sited in the United States. It also found that due to the strong statistical correlation between race and the location of hazardous wastes sites, the siting of these facilities in communities of color was no accident, but rather the intentional result of local, state, and federal land-use policies. And in 1990, sociologist Robert Bullard's *Dumping in Dixie: Race, Class, and Environmental Quality* reviewed the environmental justice struggles of several African-American communities; the stories underscored the importance of race as a factor in the siting of unwanted toxics-producing facilities.

Finding New Allies

By 1990, leaders of the growing environmental justice movement began to look for allies among the traditional, primarily white environmental organizations. These were groups that had long fought to protect wilderness, endangered species, clean air and clean water. But they had had little or no involvement in the environmental struggles of people of color under constant assault from neighboring hazardous waste landfills, waste transfer stations, incinerators, garbage dumps, diesel bus and truck garages, auto body shops, smokestack industries, industrial hog and chicken processors, oil refineries, chemical manufacturers and radioactive waste storage areas. That year, several environmental justice leaders co-signed a widely publicized letter to the "Big 10" environmental groups, including NRDC, accusing them of racial bias in policy development, hiring and the make up of their boards, and challenging them to address toxic contamination in the communities and workplaces of people of color and the poor. As a result, some mainstream environmental organizations developed their first environmental justice initiatives, added people of color to staff and resolved to take environmental justice into account when making policy decisions.

Environmental justice leaders also pushed their agenda within government. In 1990, a group of prominent academics and advocates within the movement sent letters to Louis Sullivan and

William Reilly, both top officials in the first Bush administration, to report some of their findings on the disproportionate impact of environmentally damaging facilities. The letters requested meetings to discuss needed government action. Sullivan, who is African-American, ignored the letter. Reilly accepted the offer and later that year he met with the group, a session that led to the creation of the U.S. EPA's Office of Environmental Equity.

In October 1991, the growth of the environmental justice movement became evident when the First National People of Color Environmental Leadership Summit met for three days in Washington, D.C. The summit brought together hundreds of environmental justice leaders from the United States, Canada, Central America, the Marshall Islands, and elsewhere, for the first time to network and strategize. But the list of attendees—which included Reverend Jesse Jackson, Dolores Huerta, Cherokee tribal chair Wilma Mankiller, and the heads of NRDC and the Sierra Club—also demonstrated that environmental justice was beginning to be taken up by many in the American mainstream. What's more, the summit produced the "Principles of Environmental Justice" and the "Call to Action," two foundational documents of the environmental justice movement.

National Recognition

By 1992, when Bill Clinton became president, it was clear that environmental justice was becoming important to leaders of a core constituency of the Democratic Party. Clinton appointed two environmental justice leaders, Reverend Benjamin Chavis and Dr. Robert Bullard, to his Natural Resources transition team, where they helped make environmental justice an important part of Clinton's stated environmental policy.

During the Clinton administration, environmental justice finally became federal government policy. As movement leaders from across the country looked on, including NRDC's then-director of environmental justice, Vernice Miller-Travis, President Clinton signed Executive Order 12898 in the Oval Office on February

11, 1994. The groundbreaking order directed federal agencies to identify and address disproportionately high adverse health or environmental effects of their policies or programs on low-income people and people of color. It also directed federal agencies to look for ways to prevent discrimination by race, color, or national origin in any federally funded programs dealing with health or the environment.

Today, and Tomorrow

Many grassroots environmental justice organizations have formed since the dump trucks rolled into Afton, North Carolina, more than 20 years ago. Today, many of these groups have become strong and permanent forces for environmental protection and social change in their communities:

- Concerned Citizens of South Central (Los Angeles), a housing and community development corporation that helped to lead the fight against the now infamous ANSWERS incinerator in the late 1980s, provides leadership on environmental issues and a range of other social justice issues.
- West Harlem Environmental Action was created in 1998 to fight the siting of the North River Sewage Treatment Plant, and has gone on to spearhead action on many other environmental problems in New York City and New York State.
- Through the Louisiana Avatar project under the coordination of the Deep South Center for Environmental Justice, rural parish communities in Louisiana's Cancer Alley have made major strides in publicizing, researching, and intervening in hundreds of environmental actions to protect communities from further degradation and harm.
- Mothers of East L.A., originally organized to stop the siting of a prison in the East Los Angeles community, turned its attention to opposing a hazardous waste incinerator and has subsequently taken on other local environmental and social issues.

Traditional environmental groups have also formed partnerships to support environmental justice organizations in many of their struggles. Groups such as NRDC often provide environmental justice organizations with technical advice and resources, supply expert testimony at hearings, and join in litigation. These partnerships are ongoing success stories in many parts of the country.

Environmental justice continues to be an important part of the struggle to improve and maintain a clean and healthful environment, especially for those who have traditionally lived, worked, and played closest to the sources of pollution.

2

Strategies to Fight Environmental Injustice at Home and Abroad

Robert Bullard

Robert Bullard, often described as the father of environmental justice, is Distinguished Professor of Urban Planning and Environmental Policy in the Barbara Jordan-Mickey Leland School of Public Affairs at Texas Southern University in Houston, Texas.

Environmental racism is a form of institutionalized discrimination. This excerpt asserts that it is similar to colonialism in that it distributes risk, pollution, and other negative externalities from the global North to the global South. Domestically, environmental racism is manifest as policies and agendas that expose people of color in both urban and rural areas to a host of noxious, unwanted facilities. Bullard's article delineates a paradigm to redress this system of injustice, offering tools and strategies to counter three categories of environmental racism: procedural, geographical, and social.

Anatomy of Environmental Racism

The U.S. is the dominant economic and military force in the world today. The American economic engine has generated massive wealth, high standard of living, and consumerism. This growth machine has also generated waste, pollution, and ecological destruction. The U.S. has some of the best environmental laws in the world. However, in the real world, all communities are not created equal. Environmental regulations have not achieved uniform benefits across all segments of society (Collin and Collin, 1999). Some communities are routinely poisoned while the government looks the other way.

People of color around the world must contend with dirty air and drinking water, and the location of noxious facilities such as municipal landfills, incinerators, hazardous waste treatment, storage, and disposal facilities owned by private industry, government, and even the military (Bullard, 1993a; Alston, 1993; Westra and Wentz, 1995; Robinson, 2000; Cole and Foster, 2001). These environmental problems are exacerbated by racism. *Environmental racism refers to environmental policy, practice, or directive that differentially affects or disadvantages (whether intended or unintended) individuals, groups, or communities based on race or color* (Bullard 1993a). Environmental racism is reinforced by government, legal, economic, political, and military institutions. Environmental racism combines with public policies and industry practices to provide benefits for the countries in the North while shifting costs to countries in the South (Godsil 1990; Colquett and Robertson 1991; Collin 1992; Bullard 1993a, 1999, 2000).

Environmental racism is a form of institutionalized discrimination. Institutional discrimination is defined as "actions or practices carried out by members of dominant (racial or ethnic) groups that have differential and negative impact on members of subordinate (racial and ethnic) groups" (Feagin and Feagin 1986). The United States is grounded in white racism (Doob, 1993). The nation was founded on the principles of "free land" (stolen from Native Americans and Mexicans), "free labor" (African slaves brought to this land in chains), and "free men" (only white men with property had the right to vote). From the outset, racism shaped the economic, political, and ecological landscape of this new nation.

Environmental racism buttressed the exploitation of land, people, and the natural environment. It operates as an intra-nation power arrangement—especially where ethnic or racial groups form a political and or numerical minority. For example, blacks in the U.S. form both a political and numerical racial minority. On the other hand, blacks in South Africa, under apartheid, constituted a political minority and numerical majority. American and South African apartheid had devastating environmental impacts on blacks (Kalan, 1994; Durning, 1990; South African Department of Environmental Affairs, 1996).

Environmental racism also operates in the international arena between nations and between transnational corporations. Increased globalization of the world's economy has placed special strains on the eco-systems in many poor communities and poor nations inhabited largely by people of color and indigenous peoples. This is especially true for the global resource extraction industry such as oil, timber, and minerals (Gedick, 2001; LaDuke, 1999; Karliner, 1997; Rowell, 1996). Globalization makes it easier for transnational corporations and capital to flee to areas with the least environmental regulations, best tax incentives, cheapest labor, and highest profit.

The struggle of African Americans in Norco, Louisiana, and the Africans in the Niger Delta are similar in that both groups are negatively impacted by Shell Oil refineries and unresponsive governments. This scenario is repeated for Latinos in Wilmington (California) and indigenous people in Ecuador who must contend with pollution from Texaco oil refineries (Robinson, 2000). The companies may be different, but the community complaints and concerns are very similar. Local residents have seen their air, water, and land contaminated. Many nearby residents are trapped in their community because of inadequate roads, poorly planned emergency escape routes, and faulty warning systems. They live in constant fear of plant explosions and accidents (Bullard, 2000).

The Bhopal tragedy is fresh in the minds of millions of people who live next to chemical plants. The 1984 poison-gas leak at the Bhopal, India, Union Carbide plant killed thousands of people—making it the world's deadliest industrial accident. It is not a coincidence that the only place in the U.S. where methyl isocyanate (MIC) was manufactured was at a Union Carbide plant in predominately African American Institute, West Virginia (Bullard, 2000). In 1985, a gas leak from the Institute Union Carbide plant sent 135 residents to the hospital.

Institutional racism has allowed people of color communities to exist as colonies, areas that form dependent (and unequal) relationships to the dominant white society or "Mother Country" with regard to their social, economic, legal, and environmental administration. Carmichael and Hamilton (1967), in their work *Black Power*, offered the "internal" colonial model to explain racial inequality, political exploitation, and social isolation of African Americans. Carmichael and Hamilton write:

The economic relationship of America's black communities . . . reflects their colonial status. The political power exercised over those communities go hand in glove with the economic deprivation experienced by the black citizens. Historically, colonies have existed for the sole purpose of enriching, in one form or another, the "colonizer"; the consequence is to maintain the economic dependency of the "colonized" (pp. 16-17).

Institutional racism reinforces internal colonialism. Government institutions buttress this system of domination. Institutional racism defends, protects, and enhances the social advantages and privileges of rich nations. Whether by design or benign neglect, communities of color (ranging from the urban ghettos and barrios to rural "poverty pockets" to economically impoverished Native American reservations and developing nations) face some of the worst environmental problems. The most polluted communities are also the communities with crumbling infrastructure, economic disinvestment, deteriorating housing, inadequate schools, chronic unemployment, high poverty, and overloaded health care systems (Bullard, 1996).

[...]

Environmental Justice Framework

The dominant environmental protection paradigm manages, regulates, and distributes risks (Bullard, 1996). It also institutionalizes unequal enforcement, trades human health for profit, places the burden of proof on the "victims" and not the polluting industry, legitimates human exposure to harmful chemicals, pesticides, and hazardous substances, promotes "risky" technologies, exploits the vulnerability of economically and politically disenfranchised communities, subsidizes ecological destruction, creates an industry around risk assessment and risk management, delays cleanup actions, and fails to develop pollution prevention as the overarching and dominant strategy (Bullard, 1993a, 1993b,1993c; Austin and Schill 1991).

The U.S. EPA defines environmental justice "fair treatment and meaningful involvement of all people regardless of race, color, national origin, or income with respect to the development, implementation, and enforcement of environmental laws, regulations and policies. Fair treatment means that no group of people, including racial, ethnic, or socio-economic groups should bear a disproportionate share of the negative environmental consequences resulting from industrial, municipal, and commercial operations or the execution of federal, state, local, and tribal programs and policies" (U.S. Environmental Protection Agency, 1998; Council on Environmental Quality, 1997).

In 1992, the U.S. EPA published *Environmental Equity: Reducing Risks for All Communities*— the first time the agency embarked on a systematic examination of environmental risks to communities of color (U.S. EPA, 1992). Environmental equity may mean different things to different people. Equity is distilled into three broad categories: procedural, geographic, and social equity.

Procedural equity refers to the "fairness" question: the extent that governing rules, regulations, evaluation criteria, and enforcement are applied uniformly across the board and in a nondiscriminatory way. Unequal protection might result from nonscientific and undemocratic decisions, exclusionary practices, public hearings held in remote locations and at inconvenient times, and use of English-only material as the language to communicate and conduct hearings for non-English speaking publics.

Geographic equity refers to location and spatial configuration of communities and their proximity to environmental hazards, noxious facilities, and locally unwanted land uses (LULUs) such as landfills, incinerators, sewer treatment plants, lead smelters, refineries, and other noxious facilities.

For example, unequal protection may result from land-use decisions that determine the location of residential amenities and disamenities. Unincorporated, poor, and communities of color often suffer a "triple" vulnerability of noxious facility siting.

Social Equity assesses the role of sociological factors (race, ethnicity, class, culture, life styles, political power, etc.) on environmental decision-making. Poor people and people of color often work in the most dangerous jobs, live in the most polluted neighborhoods, and their children are exposed to all kinds of environmental toxins on the playgrounds and in their homes.

The environmental justice framework rests on developing tools, strategies, and policies to eliminate unfair, unjust, and inequitable conditions and decisions (Bullard, 1996). The framework attempts to uncover the underlying assumptions that may contribute to and produce differential exposure and unequal protection. It brings to the surface the ethical and political questions of "who gets what, when, why, and how much." Some general characteristics of this framework include the following:

The environmental justice framework adopts a public health model of prevention (i.e., elimination of the threat before harm occurs) as the preferred strategy.

The environmental justice framework shifts the burden of proof to polluters/dischargers who do harm, who discriminate, or who do not give equal protection to people of color, low-income persons, and other "protected" classes.

The environmental justice framework allows disparate impact and statistical weight or an "effect" test, as opposed to "intent," to infer discrimination.

The environmental justice framework redresses disproportionate impact through "targeted" action and resources. In general, this strategy targets resources where environmental and health problems are greatest (as determined by some ranking scheme but not limited to quantitative risk assessment).

The environmental justice paradigm embraces a holistic approach to formulating environmental health policies and regulations, developing risk reduction strategies for multiple, cumulative, and synergistic risks, ensuring public health, enhancing public participation in environmental decision-making, promoting community empowerment, building infrastructure for achieving environmental justice and sustainable communities, ensuring interagency cooperation and coordination, developing innovative public/private partnerships and collaboratives, enhancing community-based pollution prevention strategies, ensuring community-based sustainable economic development, and developing geographically oriented community-wide programming.

Dumping on the Poor

Hazardous waste generation and international movement of hazardous waste still pose some important health, environmental, legal, and ethical dilemmas. The "unwritten" policy of targeting Third World nations for waste trade received international media attention in 1991. Lawrence Summers, at the time he was chief economists of the World Bank, shocked the world and touched off an international firestorm when his confidential memorandum on waste trade was leaked. Summers writes: "'Dirty' Industries: Just between you and me, shouldn't the World Bank be encouraging MORE migration of the dirty industries to the LDCs?" (Greenpeace, 1992: 1-2). Between 1989 and 1994, an estimated 2,611 metric tons of hazardous waste was exported from Organization for Economic

Cooperation and Development (OECD) countries to non-OECD countries (Greenpeace, 1994).

Transboundary Waste Trade Conventions. In a response to the growing exportation of hazardous wastes into their borders, the Organization of African Unity (OAU) and the G-77 nations mobilized to pass two important international agreements (Park, 1999). On January 30, 1991, the Pan-African Conference on Environment and Sustainable Development in Bamako, Mali, adopted the Bamako Convention on the Ban of the Import into Africa and the Control of Transboundary Movement of Hazardous wastes within Africa or the Bamako Convention (Bamako Convention, 1991).

The G-77 nations were instrumental in amending the Basel Convention to include Decision II/12, despite opposition from the United States (UNEP, 1995). On September 1995, the third Conference of Parties to the Basel Convention (COP III) approved an amendment that would ban the export of hazardous wastes from highly industrialized countries (specifically OECD countries and Lichtenstein) to all other countries (Tiemann, 1998). While Bamako and Basel may have made certain dumping formally illegal, in practice they have not prevented the transboundary movement of hazardous waste to developing countries. Loopholes still allow hazardous wastes to enter countries that do not have the resources or infrastructure to handle the wastes. For example, Karliner (1997: 152) reports that products such as pesticides and other chemicals banned or severely restricted by the United States, Western Europe, and Japan because of their acute toxicity, environmental persistence, or carcinogenic qualities are still regularly sent to the Third World. Having laws or treaties on the books and enforcing them are two different things.

Whether at home or abroad, environmental racism disadvantages people of color while providing advantages and privileges for whites. A form of illegal "exaction" forces people of color to pay costs of environmental benefits for the public at large. The question of who pays and who benefits from the current industrial and development policies is central to any analysis of environmental racism.

U.S.-Mexico Border Ecology. The conditions surrounding the more than 1,900 maquiladoras, assembly plants operated by American, Japanese, and other foreign countries, located along the 2,000-mile U.S.-Mexico border may further exacerbate the waste trade (Sanchez, 1990). The industrial plants use cheap Mexican labor to assemble imported components and raw material and then ship finished products back to the United States. Over a half million Mexican workers are employed in the maquiladoras.

All along the Lower Rio Grande River Valley maquiladoras dump their toxic wastes into the river, from which 95 percent of the region's residents get their drinking water (Hernandez, 1993). In the border cities of Brownsville, Texas, and Matamoros, Mexico, the rate of anencephaly—babies born without brains—is four times the national average. Affected families filed lawsuits against 88 of the area's 100 maquiladoras for exposing the community to xylene, a cleaning solvent that can cause brain hemorrhages, and lung and kidney damage.

The Mexican environmental regulatory agency is understaffed and ill-equipped to adequately enforce its laws (working Group on Canada-Mexico Free Trade 1991; Barry and Simms 1994). Many of the Mexican border towns have now become cities with skyscrapers and freeways. More important, the brown pallor of these southwestern skies has become a major health hazards (Barry and Simms, 1994: 37).

Radioactive Colonialism and Threatened Native Lands. There is a direct correlation between exploitation of land and exploitation of people. It should not be a surprise to anyone to discover that Native Americans have to contend with some of the worst pollution in the United States (Beasley, 1990a; Tomsho, 1990; Kay, 1991; Taliman, 1992a, 1992b). Native American nations have become prime targets for waste trading (Angel 1992; Gedicks, 1993). The vast majority of these waste proposals have been defeated by grassroots groups on the reservations. However, "radioactive colonialism" is alive and well (Churchill and LaDuke, 1983). Winona LaDuke sums up this toxic invasion of Native lands as follows: While Native peoples have been massacred and fought, cheated, and robbed of their historical lands, today their lands are subject to some of most invasive industrial interventions imaginable. According to the Worldwatch Institute, 317 reservations in the United States are threatened by environmental hazards, ranging from toxic wastes to clearcuts.

Reservations have been targeted as sites for 16 proposed nuclear waste dumps. Over 100 proposals have been floated in recent years to dump toxic waste in Indian communities. Seventy-seven sacred sites have been disturbed or desecrated through resource extraction and development activities. The federal government is proposing to use Yucca Mountain, sacred to the Shone, a dumpsite for the nation's high-level nuclear waste (LaDuke, 1999: 2–3).

Radioactive colonialism operates in energy production (mining of uranium) and disposal of wastes on Indian lands. The legacy of institutional racism has left many sovereign Indian nations without an economic infrastructure to address poverty, unemployment, inadequate education and health care, and a host of other social problems.

Some industry and governmental agencies have exploited the economic vulnerability of Indian nations. Of the twenty-one applicants for DOE's Monitored Retrievable Storage (MRS) grants, sixteen were Indian tribes (Taliman 1992). The sixteen tribes lined up for $100,000 grants from the U.S. Department of Energy (DOE) to study the prospect of "temporarily" storing nuclear waste for a half century under its "monitored retrievable storage" (MRS) program. Delegates at the Third Annual Indigenous Environmental Council Network Gathering (held in Oregon, June 6, 1992) adopted a resolution of "No Nuclear Waste on Indian Lands."

In 1999, Eastern Navajo reservation residents filed suit with the Nuclear Regulatory Commission to block a permit for uranium mining in Church Rock and Crown Point, New Mexico. The Mohave tribe in California, Skull Valley Goshutes in Idaho, and

Western Shoshone in Yucca Mountain, Nevada, are currently fighting proposals to build radioactive waste dumps on their tribal lands.

The threats to indigenous peoples are not solely confined to the United States. Native and indigenous people all across the globe are threatened with extinction due to the greed of mining and oil companies and "development genocide." Sociologist Al Gedicks's 2001 book *Resource Rebels: Native Challenges to Mining and Oil Corporations* traces the development of the grassroots multiracial transnational movement that is countering this form of environmental racism (Gedicks, 2001). Over 5,000 members of the UíWa tribe of Colombia have organized to prevent Occidental from drilling on sacred UíWa land.

The Threat from Military Toxics. Private industry does not have a monopoly on ecological threats to communities of color. War and military activities are also big players. The U.S. Department of Defense (DoD) has left its nightmarish nuclear weapons garbage on Native lands and the Pacific islands. In fact, over the last 45 years, there have been 1,000 atomic explosions on Western Shoshone land in Nevada, making the Western Shoshone the most bombed nation on earth (LaDuke, 1999: 3). The Marshall Islands residents live under a constant threat from radioactive contamination.

The military has also spoiled pristine lands in Alaska. Over 648 U.S. military installations, both active and abandoned, in Alaska are polluting the land, groundwater, wetlands, streams and air with extensive fuel spill, pesticides, solvents, PCBs, dioxins, munitions, and radioactive materials. Many of these military installations are in close proximity to Alaska Native villages and traditional hunting and fishing areas. Military toxics threaten the way of life of Alaska Natives (Miller, 2000).

Residents on the island of Vieques, Puerto Rico, are engaged in a heated battle against the U.S. Navy. The tiny island is inhabited by 9,000 residents who are bordered on both sides by the Navy. The Navy has used the U.S. commonwealth island as a bombing range since 1941. In 1999, a stray Marine Corps bomb killed a civilian security guard (Reaves and Thompson, 2001). Over 600 protesters have been arrested. Opponents contend that the bombing exercises threaten the environment and health of island residents. Several studies point to health problems which are directly related to the level of noise coming from the ship-to-shore shelling of Vieques (CNN.com, 2001).

[...]

Ecological Destruction and Corporate Welfare

The southern United States has become a "sacrifice zone" for the rest of the nation's toxic waste (Schueler, 1992). A colonial mentality exists in the Dixie where local governments and big business take advantage of people who are both politically and economically powerless. The region is stuck with a unique legacy—the legacy of slavery, Jim Crow, and white resistance to equal justice for all. This legacy has also affected race relations and the region's ecology.

The southern United States is characterized by "look-the-other-way environmental policies and giveaway tax breaks" and a place where "political bosses encourage outsiders to buy the region's human and natural resources at bargain prices" (Schueler, 1992: 46–47). Lax enforcement of environmental regulations has left the region's air, water, and land the most industry-befouled in the United States.

Ascension Parish typifies the toxic "sacrifice zone" model. In two parish towns of Geismar and St. Gabriel, 18 petrochemical plants are crammed into a nine-and-a-half-square-mile area. In Geismar, Borden Chemicals has released harmful chemicals into the environment which are health hazards to the local residents. These chemicals include ethylene dichloride, vinyl-chloride monomer, hydrogen chloride, and hydrochloric acid (Barlett and Steele 1998: 72).

Borden Chemicals has a long track record of contaminating the air, land, and water in Geismar. In March, 1997, the company paid a fine of $3.5 million, the single largest in Louisiana history. The company has been accused of storing hazardous waste, sludges, and solid wastes illegally; failing to install containment systems; burning hazardous waste without a permit; neglecting to report the release of hazardous chemicals into the air; contaminating groundwater beneath the plant site (thereby threatening an aquifer that provides drinking water for residents of Louisiana and Texas); and shipping toxic waste laced with mercury to South Africa without notifying the EPA, as required by law (Barlett and Steele, 1998).

Louisiana could actually improve its general welfare by enacting and enforcing regulations to protect the environment (Templet, 1995). However, Louisiana citizens subsidize corporate welfare with their health and the environment (Barlett and Steele, 1998). A growing body of evidence shows that environmental regulations do not kill jobs. On the contrary, the data indicate that states with lower pollution levels and better environmental policies generally have more jobs, better socioeconomic conditions and are more attractive to new business (Templet, 1995: 37). Nevertheless, some states subsidize polluting industries in the return for a few jobs (Barlett and Steele, 1998). States argue that tax breaks help create jobs. However, the few jobs that are created come at a high cost to Louisiana taxpayers and the environment.

Corporations routinely pollute Louisiana's air, ground, and drinking water while being subsidized by tax breaks from the state. The state is a leader in doling out corporate welfare to polluters (see Table 1). In the 1990s, the state wiped off the books $3.1 billion in property taxes to polluting companies. The state's top five worst polluters received $111 million dollars over the past decade (Barlett and Steele, 1998). A breakdown of the chemical releases and tax breaks include:

Cytec Industries (24.1 million pounds/$19 million tax breaks)
IMC-Agrico Co. (12.8 million pounds/$15 million tax break)
Rubicon, Inc. (8.4 million pounds of releases/$20 million)
Monsanto Co. (7.7 million pounds/$45 million)
Angus Chemical Co. (6.3 million pounds/$12 million)

Table 1: Corporate Welfare in Louisiana
The Biggest Recipients
Companies ranked by total industrial-property tax abatements

COMPANY	JOBS CREATED	TOTAL TAXES ABATED
1. Exxon Corp.	305	$213,000,000
2. Shell Chemical/Refining	167	$140,000,000
3. International Paper	172	$103,000,000
4. Dow Chemical Co.	9	$ 96,000,000
5. Union Carbide	140	$ 53,000,000
6. Boise Cascade Corp.	74	$ 53,000,000
7. Georgia Pacific	200	$ 46,000,000
8. Willamette Industries	384	$ 45,000,000
9. Procter & Gamble	14	$ 44,000,000
10. Westlake Petrochemical	150	$ 43,000,000

1988–97
The Costliest Jobs
Companies ranked by net cost of each new job
(abatements divided by jobs created)

COMPANY	JOBS CREATED	COST PER JOB
1. Mobil Oil Corp.	1	$29,100,000
2. Dow Chemical Co.	9	$10,700,000
3. Olin Corp.	5	$6,300,000
4. BP Exploration	8	$4,000,000
5. Procter & Gamble	14	$3,100,000
6. Murphy Oil USA	10	$1,600,000
7. Star Enterprise	9	$1,500,000
8. Cytec	13	$1,500,000
9. Montell USA	31	$1,200,000
10. Uniroyal Chemical Co.	22	$900,000

Source: Time *Magazine (1998)*

Subsidizing polluters is not only bad business, but it does not make environmental sense. For example, nearly three-fourths of Louisiana's population—more than 3 million people—get their drinking water from underground aquifers. Dozens of the aquifers are threatened by contamination from polluting industries (O'Byrne and Schleifstein, 1991). The Lower Mississippi River Industrial Corridor or "Cancer Alley" has over 125 companies that manufacture a range of products including fertilizers, gasoline, paints, and plastics. This corridor has been dubbed "Cancer Alley" by environmentalists and local residents (Beasley, 1990a; Bullard, 2000, Motavalli, 1998).

[…]

Residential Apartheid and Land Use

Section 24 of the South African Constitution states that "Everyone has the right: (a) to an environment that is not harmful to their health or well-being, and (b) to have the environment protected for the benefit of present and future generations." (South African Department of Environmental Affairs and Tourism, 1996: 7). The 14th Amendment to the U.S. Constitution, while [not] speaking directly to the environment, is very [much] about "equal protection for all." Nevertheless, blacks in the U.S. and blacks in South Africa have had to grapple with the legacy of legalized segregation or apartheid and dismantling "separate and unequal."

The environmental and health crisis faced by present-day South Africans originates through the combination of poor land, forced overcrowding, poverty, importation of hazardous waste, inadequate sewage, dumping of toxic chemicals into the rivers, strip mining of coal and uranium, and outdated methods of producing synthetic fuels. Apartheid herded approximately 87 percent of the black population into 13 percent of the country's territory. Such a policy spelled environmental disaster (Kalan, 1994).

Apartheid-type housing and development policies in the U.S. have resulted in limited mobility, reduced neighborhood options, decreased environmental choices, and diminished job opportunities for people of color (Bullard, Grigsby, and Lee, 1994). Race still plays a significant part in distributing public "benefits" and public "burdens" associated with economic growth.

The roots of discrimination are deep and have been difficult to eliminate. Home ownership is still a major part of the "American Dream." Housing discrimination contributes to the physical decay of inner-city neighborhoods and denies a substantial segment of African Americans and other people of color a basic form of wealth accumulation and investment through home ownership (Roisman, 1995). The number of African American homeowners would probably be higher in the absence of discrimination by lending institutions (Feagin, 1994). Only about 59 percent of the nation's middle-class African Americans own their homes, compared with 74 percent of whites.

Eight out of every ten African Americans live in neighborhoods where they are in the majority. Residential segregation decreases for most racial and ethnic groups with additional education, income, and occupational status. However, this scenario does not hold true for African Americans. African Americans, no matter what their educational or occupational achievement or income level, are exposed to higher crime rates, less effective educational systems, high mortality risks, more dilapidated surroundings, and greater environmental threats because of their race. For example, in the heavily populated South Coast air basin of the Los Angeles area, it is estimated that over 71 percent of African Americans and 50 percent of Latinos reside in areas with the most polluted air, while only 34 percent of whites live in highly polluted areas (Mann, 1991).

It has been difficult for millions of Americans in segregated neighborhoods to say "not in my backyard" (NIMBY) if they do not have a backyard. Nationally, 46.3 percent of African Americans and 36.2 percent of Latinos own their homes compared to over two-thirds of the nation as a whole. Homeowners are the strongest advocates of the NIMBY positions taken against locally unwanted land uses or LULUs such as the construction of garbage dumps, landfills, incinerators, sewer treatment plants, recycling centers, prisons, drug treatment units, and public housing projects. Generally, white communities have greater access than people of color communities when it comes to influencing land use and environmental decision making.

The ability of an individual to escape a health-threatening physical environment is usually related to affluence. However, racial and ethnic barriers complicate this process. The imbalance between residential amenities and land uses assigned to central cities and suburbs cannot be explained by class factors alone. People of color and whites do not have the same opportunities to "vote with their feet" and escape undesirable physical environments.

Institutional racism continues to influence housing and mobility options available to African Americans of all income levels—and is a major factor that influences the quality of neighborhoods they have available to them. The "web of discrimination" in the housing market is a result of action and inaction of local and federal government officials, financial institutions, insurance companies, real estate marketing firms, and zoning boards. More stringent enforcement mechanisms and penalties are needed to combat all forms of discrimination.

Some residential areas and their inhabitants are at a greater risk than the larger society from unregulated growth, ineffective regulation of industrial toxins, and public policy decisions authorizing industrial facilities that favor those with political and economic clout (Takvorian, 1993). People of color communities are often victims of land-use decision making that mirrors the power arrangements of the dominant society. Historically, exclusionary zoning (and rezoning) has been a subtle form of using government authority and power to foster and perpetuate discriminatory practices—including environmental planning.

Zoning is probably the most widely applied mechanism to regulate urban land use in the United States. Zoning laws broadly define land for residential, commercial, or industrial uses, and may impose narrower land-use restrictions (e.g., minimum and maximum lot size, number of dwellings per cre, square feet and height of buildings, etc.). Exclusionary zoning has been used to zone against something rather than for something. On the other hand, "expulsive" zoning has pushed out residential and allowed "dirty" industries to invade communities (Bullard, 2000). Largely the poor, people of color, and renters inhabit the most vulnerable communities. With or without zoning, deed restrictions or other devices, various groups are unequally able to protect their environmental interests. More often than not, people of color communities get shortchanged in the neighborhood protection game.

Zoning ordinances, deed restrictions, and other land-use mechanisms have been widely used as a "NIMBY" (not in my backyard) tool, operating through exclusionary practices. In Houston, Texas, the only major American city that does not have zoning, NIMBY was replaced with the policy of "PIBBY" (place in blacks' backyard). The city government and private industry targeted landfills, incinerators, and garbage dumps for Houston's black neighborhoods for more than five decades (Bullard, 1983, 1987). These practices lowered residents' property values, accelerated physical deterioration, and increased disinvestment. Moreover, the discriminatory siting of landfills and incinerators stigmatized Houston neighborhoods as "dumping grounds" for a host of other unwanted facilities, including salvage yards, recycling operations, and automobile "chop shops."

3

Flint's Water Crisis Fits a Pattern of Environmental Injustice

Jean Ross

Jean Ross was former Program Officer, Civic Engagement and Government, Ford Foundation.

Flint, Michigan, recently found itself under emergency management in the wake of budgetary problems. To save money, the city sourced water from the heavily polluted Flint River instead of Lake Huron, dismissing the many health concerns of citizens. Journalist Curt Guyette exposed this story to national attention, and now Flint is finally on the road to recovery. The episode is a cautionary tale for municipalities considering unethical ways to save money at the expense of public health.

B y now, the consequences of the disastrous decision to shift the source of the city of Flint, MI's water supply are well known. The public outcry generated by almost daily headline coverage of the crisis has led to some urgent and essential actions—such as distributing bottled water and monitoring children exposed to high levels of lead—as well as conversations about the need for a permanent solution. But for that solution to be a meaningful and lasting one, we need to look back to the roots of the problem.

"The Crisis In Flint Is About More Than Poisoned Water," Jean Ross, Ford Foundation, February 2, 2016, https://www.fordfoundation.org/ideas/equals-change-blog/posts/the-crisis-in-flint-is-about-more-than-poisoned-water/. Licensed under CC BY 4.0 International.

Where the Crisis Came From

In the spring of 2013, the city of Detroit and other Michigan communities—including Flint—faced serious budget shortfalls and struggling economies. The governor appointed an emergency manager to guide Detroit through bankruptcy, using powers provided by a law that replaced a measure voters had recently repealed. Anger, distrust, and tensions ran high, for good reason: Critical decisions that would shape the city's future for decades to come would be made largely behind closed doors, by an appointed official who answered to the governor, not local voters. And the fiscal crises facing Detroit and nearby communities continued to escalate.

Due to ongoing budget problems, nearby Flint was also under the control of an emergency manager. In April 2014, as a cost-saving measure, the emergency manager terminated a contract that had provided the city with clean water from Lake Huron, in favor of sourcing water from the Flint River. Immediately, residents complained about the color, taste, and smell of the water from the new source—and, when the shift led to a hike in water rates, about its cost. State and local officials rebuffed their critics and denied that any problem existed.

Uncovering the Truth

Lacking traditional ways of ensuring transparency and accountability—like residents testifying at a public meeting, or local officials taking a public vote—advocates faced a serious challenge: How could they bring attention to the crisis? As part of a watchdog effort focused on state-appointed emergency managers, a grant from Ford funded the work of journalist Curt Guyette, hired by the ACLU of Michigan to investigate how the decisions of emergency managers were impacting financially strapped Michigan communities. That assignment brought Guyette to Flint, where through dogged reporting he was able to draw awareness not only to the water crisis, but also to the lack of transparent and accountable government in Michigan.

Working with researchers and activists, Guyette ferreted out critical documents that validated residents' complaints and showed a callous indifference to public health and safety. His work drew sorely needed attention to the crisis, and has helped start a national conversation about accountability, transparency, and what citizens deserve from their governments. It also provided fuel for a lawsuit filed by the ACLU and allies against the City of Flint and the state for violations of the federal Safe Drinking Water Act. As a result of his groundbreaking coverage, last week the Michigan Press Association named Guyette Michigan Journalist of the Year.

A Broken System

In the short term, we know what to do about the water crisis: Distribute bottled water, and change the water source. But once those most immediate problems are addressed, we're left with the same system that helped create the problem, and it continues to reinforce inequalities that shape the lives of people in Flint. The use of emergency managers has been largely reserved for cities with majority-black populations, where residents find their lives presided over by officials who are more concerned with financial health than public wellbeing. That's what led to the water crisis. Emergency manager control has also limited residents' ability to participate in decisions about how to fix public schools in Detroit and other communities that are close to financial collapse.

Today, the city of Detroit has returned to local control and the city of Flint is on the road to securing a safe water supply. But there is a long way to go in restoring the public's confidence in government. Not least of all, the law that allowed the disastrous decision about water supply to be made without public scrutiny remains on the books. Efforts to strengthen the voices and influence of local residents persist. Without governance that is truly responsive, representative, and accountable, journalists like Curt Guyette will continue to have lots to report on. So what can we do to rebuild the kind of diverse, engaged civic fabric that is so important to a healthy community, and so necessary to hold elected leaders to account?

Justice, Clean Water, and Good Governance

Against the stark background, there is reason for optimism. A new generation of civic activism and engagement is building collaboration among diverse Detroit communities, united by a fierce commitment to securing a better future for this once great American city. Already, we've seen activists working together on a plan to return Detroit Public Schools to local control and foster academic excellence, and to educate voters about the city's new system of district election. And we see emerging efforts to develop leaders and organizations that can achieve change at home and build the networks that are needed to start a new statewide policy debate. All of these efforts can serve as a blueprint for the residents of Flint as they pursue justice, clean water, and the governance they deserve.

4

Religious Voices Play a Critical Role in Environmental Justice

Julia Watts Belser

Julia Watts Belser is assistant professor of Judaism in the religious studies department at Missouri State University.

The environmental justice movement was led in large part by members of the United Church of Christ. In a sense, then, religion has been the backbone of efforts to correct incidents of environmental racism. In this viewpoint, Julia Watts Belser argues the importance of viewing environmental injustices interreligiously, from the perspective of a variety of religions. This includes non-Christian religions.

When I begin a new course on "Religion and the Environment," most students come to class assuming religious environmentalism is primarily concerned with "protecting nature." They are almost uniformly startled when we begin by studying the Bhopal gas tragedy—the 1984 industrial–environmental catastrophe in which forty tons of toxic gas exploded from a poorly maintained Union Carbide pesticide factory, killing thousands of residents and exposing some of India's poorest communities to devastating health consequences that continue to this day. The case draws critical attention to the brutal body costs of neocolonialism and corporate irresponsibility, centering our gaze on the race,

"Environmental Justice and Interreligious Ecotheology," Julia Watts Belser, Religious Studies News, March 15, 2013. http://rsn.aarweb.org/spotlight-on/theo-ed /environemental-justice/environmental-justice-and-interreligious-ecotheology. Licensed under CC BY-SA 2.0.

class, and gender disparities of environmental violence. As students examine the grassroots response and chronicle the ongoing efforts to secure compensation for survivors, we frame a key question that grounds the course: *How do religious responses to environmental crisis engage with—or turn away from—the ethical demands of environmental injustice?*

Religious voices have played a critical role in birthing the environmental justice movement. In 1982, a grassroots movement led in large part by African-American church women protested the placement of a toxic waste landfill in a poor, predominantly black community in Warren County, North Carolina. In 1987, the United Church of Christ's Commission for Racial Justice published a landmark study, "Toxic Waste and Race," that chronicled the disproportionate toxic exposures born by U.S. communities of color—three out of five black and Hispanic Americans live in communities with an uncontrolled toxic waste site, as do half of all Asians/Pacific Islanders and Native Americans. Active community organizing has led to some progress, but a 2007 follow-up report by the United Church of Christ shows that environmental racism and injustice continue to remain entrenched patterns.

Yet within the academy, religious studies scholars and theologians have often paid less explicit attention to the intersections of justice, violence, and environmental harm. This issue of *Spotlight on Theological Education* asks how educators can more critically engage questions of justice as we teach ecotheology and religious environmentalism. The issue cultivates strategies and reflections for more thoroughly integrating race, gender, and class into environmental theology. It calls for an engagement with disability studies, attending to the increasing realities of environmentally induced disability and challenging the perception of disability as a solely individual experience. It highlights the importance of creative ritual as a tool for cultivating ecotheological insight and commitment. It also calls attention to the importance of thinking interreligiously about environmental theology—lifting up the theological insights of scholars writing from non-Christian traditions.

Larry Rasmussen's essay asks how religious communities and theological educators can help us better prepare for life in the Anthropocene era, an era of rapid human-induced planetary change. Rasmussen lays out the transitions that humanity must undertake to become a viable species, living lives of mutual enhancement with all other living beings. He suggests that religious communities can be central to this transformation in culture and consciousness if religious ritual, symbolism, and practice are reimagined and revisioned for a new ecological age. Rasmussen reflects here on the pedagogy of "Earth-honoring Faith," a ten-year project at Ghost Ranch that brings together clergy, lay leaders, and scholars to cultivate multidisciplinary knowledge and critical religious imagination in order to develop new ecoreligious practice. He calls on religious communities to embrace the task of planet-keeping and the moral obligations of creation justice.

While Rasmussen calls for creation justice to become "a common calling" that unites religious communities, Cynthia Moe-Lobeda highlights the problem of privilege that makes certain communities simultaneously able to benefit from, and distance themselves from, the most overt costs of environmental harm. She argues that the present state of widespread moral oblivion to climate change represents a devastating and far-reaching example of white privilege and class privilege. Moe-Lobeda examines the pedagogical challenges of theological education that draws students' critical attention to environmental injustice. Her essay shares teaching strategies for developing a three-part moral vision:

- Analyzing the problems of power and the realities of injustice
- Attending to the sustainable alternatives and resistance movements that are present, but rarely acknowledged in dominant discourse
- Cultivating an awareness of Spirit that inclines toward justice and draws us to abundant life for all people and all beings

Engaging the ongoing grassroots struggles for environmental justice, Melanie L. Harris grounds her essay in the powerful legacies of African-American women's protests against environmental racism. She lays out the theoretical framework of ecowomanist thought, emphasizing that the Womanist commitment to survival and wholeness demands an integrated response to racism, sexism, and environmental devastation. Harris aims to help students make connections between race, economics, gender, sex, and earth justice. Reflecting on her own pedagogy, she often juxtaposes ecotheology and environmental ethics with the work of ecoliterary authors such as Alice Walker. Harris also calls attention to the power of ritual in and beyond the classroom as a method for helping students transform their learning into a lived commitment to environmental justice.

Sharon V. Betcher's essay examines the importance of integrating disability into our analysis of ecotheology and environmental justice. Bridging her scholarship in disability studies and her work in environmental studies, Betcher emphasizes that environmental devastation is increasingly causing disablement. In the Anthropocene era, she argues that environmentally induced disability is a form of human-on-human violence and a manifestation of our violence against the earth. Yet she resists the move to position disability solely as a "scare tactic" designed to promote better ecological citizenship. In contrast to the prevailing tendency to view disability as an individual tragedy marked by pathos and personal suffering, Betcher argues that disability is one form of bodily responsiveness to the vagaries and complexities of embodied life. She calls us to reconceptualize disablement in communal terms, to think of how we are collectively affecting our common human flesh, and to attend to the way the elements of life speak to and through our bodies.

Centering attention on the problem of violence that has surfaced in several earlier essays, Pankaj Jain raises up the Hindu, Jain, and Buddhist commitment to ahimsa (nonviolence) as a critical environmental value. He calls for Western environmentalists and theologians to learn from the example of Gandhi and the wisdom of the Indic traditions, emphasizing the importance of grounding ecological action in the principles and practice of nonviolence. Jain chronicles the work of Indian activists, reformers, and community leaders whose commitment to ahimsa inspires them to resist violence and imperialism, to counter pressures for rampant industrialism and consumerism, and to improve the well-being of earth, humans, and all beings.

Where Jain critiques the West's tendency to "make war" on everything, from climate change to terrorism, Sandra B. Lubarsky challenges the Western inclination to turn away from beauty. Accentuating the premodern conviction that the beauty of creation reflects and expresses the nature of God, Lubarsky links the modern disinterest in beauty with the disenchantment of the world. Beauty, she suggests, can inspire our environmental concern and draw us more fully into the life of the world. Returning full circle to Rasmussen's call to transform our worldviews by reimagining religious ritual, Lubarsky highlights the ecological potential of the Jewish practice of hiddur mitzvah, embellishing and beautifying the commandments. Refashioning this practice as a touchstone to increase our awareness of and appreciation for earth's beauty, she suggests that an obligation to cultivate beauty urges us to look beyond ourselves—drawing us to participate in and enhance the beauty and well-being of earth and all creation.

By centering on new directions in ecology and theology, these essays invite readers to more fully integrate concern for justice into ecological theologies and pedagogies. They ask readers to consider anew the potential and power of religious ritual in places of worship, at protest sites, and in the classroom. And they call for renewed commitment to interreligious teaching and learning as we engage in the critical practice of ecotheology and ecojustice.

5

The Food Industry Is Complicit with Environmental Racism

Food Empowerment Project

Food Empowerment Project seeks to create a more just and sustainable world by recognizing the power of one's food choices. We encourage choices that reflect a more compassionate society by spotlighting the abuse of animals on farms, the depletion of natural resources, unfair working conditions for produce workers, the unavailability of healthy foods in communities of color and low-income areas, and the importance of not purchasing chocolate that comes from the worst forms of child labor.

Factory farming is obviously bad for animals. Although many are coming to agree it is bad for humans too, we typically do not consider how our system of food production impacts some people more adversely than others. Much like waste treatment plants and other hazards, industrial food producers locate their polluting plants and Controlled Animal Feeding Operations (CAFOs) in areas that are primarily inhabited by the poor and people of color. This makes them part of the problem of environmental racism. Ethical and informed food choices can mitigate some of these ill effects.

While pollution is almost everywhere, certain communities are burdened with a disproportionate number of facilities that fill the air, soil, and water with contaminates. Typically found

"Environmental Racism," Food Empowerment Project. www.foodispower.org. Reprinted by permission.

in communities of color and low-income communities, industrial polluters such as landfills, trash incinerators, coal plants, and toxic waste dumps affect the well being of residents. Their health is also often compromised due to a lack of access to healthy foods in their neighborhoods. Those who work on environmental justice issues refer to these inequities as environmental racism.

Environmental Justice activists approach environmental protection in a different way than those groups that focus solely on environmental issues. These activists consider the environment to be where "we live, work and play, go to school (and sometimes pray)." They act to right the wrongs of environmental racism, which is typically due to the intended or unintended consequences of regulations that may be selectively enforced or not enforced at all, resulting in negative impacts on people of color.

When they hear about industrial pollution, people often think about factories with billowing smokestacks. However, the food industry, with its factory farms and slaughterhouses, can also be considered a major contributor of pollution that affects the health of communities of color and low-income communities, because more often than not they locate their facilities in the areas where these people live. "Swine CAFOs [Confined Animal Feeding Operations] are disproportionately located in communities of color and regions of poverty ..." say Maria C. Mirabelli, Steve Wing, Stephen W. Marshall, and Timothy C. Wilcosky of the School of Public Health at the University of North Carolina-Chapel Hill.[1]

Among the corporations that harm the environment and the health of communities of color and low-income communities are those that run industrial pig farms. Research has shown that these pig farms are responsible for both air and water pollution, mostly due to the vast manure lagoons they create to hold the enormous amount of waste from the thousands of pigs being raised for food. Residents who live near these factory farms often complain of irritation to their eyes, noses, and throats, along with a decline in the quality of life and increased incidents of depression, tension, anger, confusion, and fatigue.[2]

In North Carolina, it has been said that the number of pigs on factory farms exceeds the total population of people in the state. The contamination from North Carolina pig farms has yielded dangerous concentrations of groundwater nitrates, a leading cause of blue baby syndrome. Hydrogen sulfide has also caused noticeable increases in respiratory ailments near these sites. And because of the location of these industrialized farms, those affected most are low-income communities of color.[3]

This is not an isolated example. The placement of these facilities is not always an intentional process on the part of industry leaders. Instead, because of the distinct connections between ethnicity and class in the United States, poor rural areas tend to house communities of color and the land in these areas is cheaper. According to sociologists Bob Bolin, Sara Grineski, and Timothy Collins of Arizona State University, "Land use, housing segregation, racialized employment patterns, financial practices, and the way that race permeates zoning, development, and bank lending processes" are also fundamental drivers of environmental racism.[4] North Carolina is one example, but similar patterns exist in most major agricultural areas.[3]

Corporations may also locate to these rural areas either believing that the residents do not have the political will and won't present obstacles, or that these low-income residents need the jobs and will not complain. Environmental Justice activists consider the latter reason to be a form of economic extortion— having to accept the negative health consequences and adverse effects on the environment in order to have a job. This scenario is fortunately not a given with more frequent challenges being made to these injustices.

What is often overlooked, however, is the harm being done to the surrounding communities, with generation after generation suffering illnesses caused by the industrial pollution of the land, air and water. The risk to the health of residents depends on rates of exposure. Workers and their families are the most severely affected, but community health is also a big concern. Runoff from factory farms—containing a wide range of pathogens, antibiotics, and other toxic chemicals—can permeate aquifers and contaminate surrounding groundwater sources. Viruses can be transmitted from the workers in these facilities to their families and communities. Moreover, undocumented workers in meatpacking facilities and factory farms are often less willing to participate in health programs that are in place for fear of legal consequences.[5]

Air pollution also poses risks to vulnerable members of populations near factory farms, specifically children, the elderly, and individuals with pre-existing respiratory diseases. In particular, epidemiological studies on factory farm emissions show strong correlations between these pollutants and asthma. The results from surveys of rural North Carolina schools also showed strong correlations between asthma diagnoses and proximity to factory farms. Schools with a significant number of students of color (about 37%) and slightly less than half of the student bodies on reduced lunch programs were located an average of 4.9 miles from pig factory farms, yet schools with more white and higher-income students were found to be an average of 10.8 miles away. Significant correlations were also found between race, poverty, and the odor exposure from these pig factory farms.[1]

California's dairy industry is also no exception. More than 1.5 million cows can be found in the state, with most living on mega dairy farms. There is no question that dairy factory farms contribute to air pollution, and the Environmental Protection Agency has been researching just how much factory farms do contribute.[6]

Many of these industrialized animal factories are concentrated in the San Joaquin Valley, an agricultural region that stretches from Stockton to Bakersfield, and from 2001 to 2005 there was a 3% increase in the number of residents with asthma.[7] As of 2005, more than one in five children living in the San Joaquin Valley had asthma, with Fresno County being called the asthma capital of California, where almost one in three children are asthmatic.[8] "Car and diesel exhaust, dairy farm waste, agricultural field dust, pesticides, and industrial soot provide the raw ingredients for the Valley's dirty air," reports the Fresno Bee.[8] It is therefore not surprising that these factory farms are located in the vicinity of a large number of communities of color living in poverty. According to a recent report by the Central Policy Health Institute: "In 2005, seven of the eight San Joaquin Valley counties had a higher percentage of Latino residents than the state as a whole (35.9%)."[9] The report adds that the San Joaquin Valley is "one of the least affluent areas of California…and poverty, in both urban and rural areas, is a significant problem."[9]

Water pollution is another major factor for those living in agricultural areas where the residents "rely on groundwater from community wells that are often contaminated with pesticides, animal waste and fertilizer byproducts."[10] It is not uncommon for nitrate, a chemical found in both animal manure and nitrogen-based fertilizer, to pass through the soil and contaminate local groundwater. Research done by doctoral candidate Carolina Balazs at UC Berkeley found that, "In California, the majority of people exposed to nitrate-contaminated water live in the San Joaquin Valley…with a disproportionate exposure among predominantly Latino communities."[10] According to Balazs' preliminary research results, "communities that have the worst water quality are 65 percent Latino and 50 percent are near or below the poverty line."[10]

It is tragic that these communities often do not have access to alternate means of earning an income or to alternatives to animal products or contaminated tap water. They are hurt by the system and have few reasonable choices. Such limitations are an integral part of the factory farming system. With consumers continuing to demand high amounts of factory-farmed "meat," communities—not just workers, but entire communities—will continue to be hit hardest by pollution and toxins. Certainly plant foods may also be tied to toxic chemical use and abuse as well, but given the huge quantities of plants needed to feed animals raised for food, choosing vegan options goes a long way in reducing our collective "pollution footprints." Our daily meals offer us the chance to vote with our dollars and stand in solidarity with communities against environmental racism. Environmental racism may take many forms, but when it comes to injustices directly linked to the food industry, we can do our part to not contribute to these unjust actions by choosing a vegan diet.

References

1 Maria C. Mirabelli, Steve Wing, Stephen W. Marshall, and Timothy C. Wilcosky, "Race, Poverty, and Potential Exposure of Middle-School Students to Air Emissions from Confined Swine Feeding Operations," n.d., http://www.ncbi.nlm.nih.gov/pmc/articles /PMC1440786/ (12/4/10)

2 David Wallinga, M.D., Institute for Agricultural Trade Policy, "Concentrated Animal Feeding Operations: Health Risks from Air Pollution" (2004) Retrieved 3/15/2013 fromhttp://www.iatp.org/documents/concentrated-animal-feeding-operations-health -risks-from-air-pollution

3 "The Industrialization of Agriculture and Environmental Racism: A Deadly Combination Affecting Neighborhoods and the Dinner Table," July 30, 1997. Retrieved 3/18/2013 fromhttp://www.iatp.org/files/Industrialization_of_Agriculture_and _Environme.htm

4 B. Bolin, S. Grineski, and T. Collins, "The Geography of Despair; Environmental Racism and the Making of South Phoenix, Arizona, USA," Human Ecology Review 12, no. 2 (2005): 156.

5 Putting Meat on the Table: Industrial Farm Animal Production in America (Pew Commission on Industrial Farm Animal Production, April 2008), http://www.ncifap.org (12/10/10)

6 "Air Emissions Monitoring Study." US Environmental Protection Agency. http://www .epa.gov/agriculture/airmonitoringstudy.html#data (4/12/13)

7 Lisa Kresge, Ron Strochlic, "Clearing the Air: Mitigating the Impact of Dairies on Fresno County's Air Quality and Public Health," Retrieved 3/15/2013 from http://www.ncfh.org /pdfs/6940.pdf

8 Fresno Bee, Barbara Anderson, Fresno is State's Asthma Capital, 2007 http://www .fresnobee.com/2007/12/12/v-printerfriendly/263218/fresno-is-states-asthma-capital .html(12/12/10)

9 Bengiamin, M., Capitman, J.A., and Chang, X. (2008). Healthy people 2010: A 2007 profile of health status in the San Joaquin Valley. Fresno, CA: California State University, Fresno. Retrieved 3/18/2013 from http://www.fresnostate.edu/chhs/ccchhs/documents /healthy-people-2010-2007-profile.pdf

10 San Joaquin Valley residents express their concern over drinking water contamination, Eyal Matalon, El Tecolote June 2010 http://eltecolote.org/content/2010/06/san-joaquin -valley-residents-express-their-concern-over-drinking-water-contamination/ (12/12/10)

6

Government Response to Environmental Hazards in Minority Communities Is Too Slow

Ryan Schwier and Peter Elliott

Ryan Schwier has clerked for the Indiana Attorney General and is health law and policy fellow at LUNA Language Services. Peter Elliott is an attorney in the Indiana Commercial Court.

The following excerpt serves as the introduction to a collaborative project created by law students at the Indiana University Robert H. McKinney School of Law, for a semester-long course taught by Prof. Carlton Waterhouse during the fall of 2014. The authors provide a broad introduction to the environmental justice movement in the United States, including the key people and events that defined the movement, before zeroing in on contemporary developments in the state of Indiana. Their purpose is to illustrate patterns of historical environmental inequities in an effort to address similar injustices today.

National Origins

During the early 1980s, the United States witnessed a new environmental campaign taking shape—one rooted in the civil rights and anti-toxics movements of previous decades. In September of 1982, the residents of Warren County, North Carolina, marched in protest against the siting of a local polychlorinated biphenyl

(PCB) landfill. Four years prior, over 30,000 gallons of waste oil contaminated with PCBs were illegally discharged onto roadsides across the state. After the Environmental Protection Agency (EPA) designated these sites for remedial cleanup, the state needed a place to dispose of the contaminated soil. In 1979, the North Carolina Department of Environmental and Natural Resources chose the rural, poor, and predominantly black Warren County for the landfill. The local NAACP filed suit in an attempt to block the landfill, but ultimately failed. The first trucks to arrive at the site met with sharp protest, resulting in hundreds of arrests.

Soon, communities across the United States followed suit. Residents from predominantly low-income, minority communities—from Chester, Pennsylvania, and Camden, New Jersey, to Los Angeles, California, and the small parishes along the Mississippi River between Baton Rouge and New Orleans—protested local government decisions to license the siting or expansion of landfills, hazardous waste facilities, and other environmentally unfriendly land uses near their homes. Through grassroots organizing and civil rights activism, the quest for environmental justice had begun.

Defining the Movement

The environmental justice movement emerged in response to an alarming amount of evidence that low-income communities of color are not only burdened with a disproportionate share of environmental hazards, but also less likely to enjoy the environmental and human health benefits of parks, recreation, public sanitation, and other quality-of-life factors because of expense or disproportionate allocation of public resources. So the question arises: is the environmental justice movement concerned with ecological preservation (i.e., going "green") or the promotion of public health?

Traditional environmental organizations such as the Sierra Club, Natural Resources Defense Council, and National Wildlife Federation—while distinguished from each other by unique goals and practices—share a common history that extends from the "back-to-nature" principles of the 19th-century conservation movement. In response to rapid industrialization of the nation's urban centers, conservationists such as John Muir and Gifford Pinchot sought to prevent what they considered the imminent loss of the nation's natural resources. With a cynical eye toward the indiscriminately wasteful practices of American industry, these early conservationists viewed the city as an environmental nuisance rather than a potential solution to ecological degradation. In short, the conservation movement of the late-nineteenth century "had no place in its nature-focused ethos for direct confrontation with urban life and no consideration for the problems of the poor, much less the problems of the people of color."

As the conservation movement gained force, urban living conditions during the late-19th century, which deteriorated rapidly from industrial pollution and the failure of public sanitary systems to accommodate an increasingly dense urban society, stimulated a growing public health movement in the United States. Unlike the conservation movement, the campaign for public health made a distinct connection between the environment (both natural and built) and the physical well being of humans. While distinctions between the two movements have, in recent decades, become blurred—especially in areas related to lead poisoning, municipal water treatment, and air quality—an anti-urban bias continues to pervade the underlying philosophy of the major environmental organizations today.

With its health and human-oriented approach, environmental justice emphasizes the interaction between the physical and natural world. In this sense, "environment" concerns not only the ecological preservation of natural resources, but also the protection of healthy living spaces—the daily settings where people live, work, play, worship, and go to school. Accordingly, EJ advocates seek to prevent environmental threats in housing, land use, industrial sitings, health care, and public sanitation services.

The Federal Response

In response to the events of Warren County and mounting concerns over environmental inequity, several studies were conducted to examine the siting of environmentally hazardous landfills and the demographics of the host communities. In 1983, following congressional approval, the U.S. Government Accountability Office (U.S. GAO) released *Siting of Hazardous Waste Landfills and Their Correlation with Racial and Economic Status of Surrounding Communities*. The study revealed that 3 of 4 off-site commercial hazardous waste landfills in the EPA's Region 4 (composed of 8 southern states) were located in predominantly African-American communities, although African-Americans made up only 20% of the region's population. Four years later, the United Church of Christ Commission for Racial Justice (CCCRJ) published *Toxic Waste and Race in the United States*. The investigation found that race was the most potent variable in predicting where waste facilities would be located—more powerful than poverty, land values, and home ownership.

Executive Order 12898

In 1994, President Bill Clinton issued Executive Order 12898, Federal Actions to Address Environmental Justice in Minority Populations and Low-Income Populations. With a goal of achieving environmental protection for all communities, the Executive Order places special emphasis on the environmental and human health effects of federal action on of minority and low-income populations. In meeting these ends, the Order specified the creation of an Interagency Working Group on Environmental Justice, directed research and analysis of human health and environmental hazards, and underscored public participation and access to information in the environmental decision-making process.

The Presidential Memorandum accompanying the Order highlights existing laws to "ensure that all communities and persons across th[e] Nation live in a safe and healthful environment." Specifically, the memo focused on Title VI of the Civil Rights

Act of 1964 and the National Environmental Policy Act (NEPA). Title VI prohibits discrimination on the basis of race, color, and national origin in programs and activities receiving federal financial assistance. NEPA requires federal agencies to consider the environmental impacts of their proposed actions and reasonable alternatives to those actions. Procedural provisions under NEPA further require periods for public commenting, which the lead federal agency proposing the action must consider in the planning process.

Environmental Justice at the EPA

In 1998, the EPA established its own definition of environmental justice, which embraces "the fair treatment and meaningful involvement of all people regardless of race, color, national origin, or income with respect to the development, implementation, and enforcement of environmental laws, regulations, and policies." Further, the "goal for all communities and persons across this Nation . . . will be achieved when everyone enjoys the same degree of protection from environmental and health hazards and equal access to the decision-making process to have a healthy environment in which to live, learn, and work."

Progress and Impediments

The explicit recognition of environmental inequities by the federal executive provided the EJ movement with a strong sense of accomplishment. Yet despite these promising measures, other developments severely limited genuine environmental equality as a matter of law and policy. In 1992, Representative John Lewis and Senator Al Gore proposed the Environmental Justice Act. The bill (H.R. 2105, 103rd Cong.) was intended to "establish a program to assure nondiscriminatory compliance with all environmental, health and safety laws and to assure equal protection of the public health." Despite the support of 44 co-sponsors, the bill died following a series of subcommittee hearings. The following year, the Act was redrafted and reintroduced (S. 1161, 103rd Cong.)

by Representative Lewis and Senator Max Baucus. Again, the bill died after committee referral.

Beyond the federal legislative arena, environmental justice claimants have encountered mixed results in the courts. The majority of successful claims originate in traditional common law nuisance theories or under environmental laws such as the National Environmental Protection Act. On the other hand, claims alleging equal protection violations under the Fourteenth Amendment have largely failed because of the high evidentiary burden of proving racial motivation or discriminatory intent. Despite recommendations set forth in the Clinton Memorandum, complaints alleging disparate impact discrimination on the basis of race in violation of Title VI of the Civil Rights Act of 1964 have likewise proven futile. In 2001, the U.S. Supreme Court held in *Alexander v. Sandoval*, 525 U.S. 275, that no private right of action existed to enforce disparate-impact regulations promulgated under Title VI.

At the federal administrative level, the EPA has been particularly slow in developing a framework for investigating and acting upon claims of discrimination. In addition, a 1992 investigation by the *National Law Journal* revealed compelling evidence of racially inequitable enforcement of federal laws and cleanup efforts by the EPA.

Indiana

Indiana's environmental justice program took shape in 1996. That year, EPA's Region 5 (which, in addition to Indiana, includes the states of Illinois, Michigan, Minnesota, Ohio, Wisconsin, and 35 Native American tribes) designated northwest Indiana as one of its "geographic initiatives." According to Region 5's 1996 *Agenda for Action*:

> Northwest Indiana, spanning the southern shore of Lake Michigan, has experienced a century of severe environmental degradation. This is largely because of the steel and petroleum refining industries, because of alteration of the natural ecosystem

by filling of dunes and wetlands, and because of overall development. Ozone and particulate nonattainment, 10 million cubic yards of contaminated sediments in the Indiana Harbor Ship Canal and the Grand Calumet River, millions of gallons of free-floating petroleum products in the ground-water, and numerous sites contaminated with hazardous waste—including 15 Superfund sites—are some of the many environmental challenges facing the area.

In October of the following year, the EPA announced the winners of its Environmental Justice Community/University Partnership Grants, which allocated over $2 million to eleven individual projects throughout the United States. According to the EPA press release:

> The program was established to help minorities and low-income communities address local environmental justice issues through formal partnership agreements with colleges or universities. The winners have created projects that will increase environmental awareness, expand community outreach and provide training and education to socio-economically disadvantaged communities impacted by environmental hazards.

Among the grant recipients was Indiana University Northwest, which used the funds to establish the Northwest Indiana Environmental Justice partnership and Resource Center (EJRC). The mission of the EJRC was to (1) research evidence of an environmental "disproportionate impact" on core urban communities in Northwest Indiana; (2) create a partnership between IU Northwest and community organizations concerned with environmental issues in the urban core of northwestern Indiana; and (3) provide residents with information and data relating to environmental issues in urban areas of the region. Although the EPA grant ended in 2003, the Center continued for several years to facilitate EJ activities in the region through funding from the IU Northwest Library Data Center.

In 1998, IDEM received an EPA environmental justice grant, providing the momentum for a state-wide initiative. Two years

later, the Indianapolis Urban League's Environmental Coalition—
the recipient of an environmental justice "small grant" from the
EPA—published a study on the relationship between race, income,
and toxic air releases. The study, which further prompted IDEM
to address EJ issues, concluded that

> [b]oth low-income residents and black residents (who make up
> 90 percent of the minority population) are disproportionately
> located near TRI (toxic release inventory) facilities in
> Indianapolis, Indiana. As a result, these populations may face
> greater health risks from hazardous air emissions.

In 2000, IDEM convened the Interim Environmental Justice
Advisory Council—a stakeholder-based group comprised of
citizens, environmentalists, academics, and industry representatives
from across the state—to assist in developing an EJ Strategic Plan.
The Plan, adopted in August 2001, offered a vision statement:
"No citizens or communities of the state of Indiana, regardless
of race, color, national origin, income or geographic location,
will bear a disproportionate share of the risk and consequences
of environmental pollution or will be denied equal access to
environmental benefits."

In fulfilling this vision, the agency's mission statement
specified that IDEM collaborate with state communities to ensure
development and implementation of policies, programs, and
procedures that

- Inform, educate and empower all people in our state to
  have meaningful participation in decisions which affect
  their environment;
- Reduce any cumulative disparate impact of environmental
  burden, including burdens from past practices, on people
  of color and/or low-income status; and
- Address IDEM's obligations under Title VI of the Civil Rights
  Act of 1964.

The Plan also contained several goals, including: (1)
identification of geographic areas of EJ concern; (2) community

education on EJ issues, public participation in environmental decision-making, and the agency's statutory responsibilities; (3) ensuring opportunities for affected parties to communicate their concerns to IDEM on facility permitting and other decisions involving EJ issues; (4) IDEM staff education; (5) evaluation, with community input, of the effectiveness and appropriateness of existing public processes for environmental decision-making; and (6) involvement of other state agencies (e.g., Indiana Department of Transportation) in EJ discussions to assist in developing their own programs.

Other IDEM initiatives utilizing the EPA EJ grant included GIS mapping, a *Guide to Citizen Participation* (originally published in English and Spanish), and a brochure on *How to Participate in Environmental Decision-Making.* The agency's EJ mapping project—which used census data on the state's demographics and GIS software to collect information on Superfund sites and hazardous waste facilities—helped identify the proximity of low-income and minority residents to environmental hazards.

In 2006, IDEM adopted its first environmental justice policy. The policy, amended in 2008, identifies EJ as including the "fair treatment and meaningful involvement of all people in the implementation of environmental decision-making pursuant to all Federal and State environmental statutes, regulations and rules." Accordingly, IDEM endeavors to ensure that all members of the public have (1) equal access to pertinent agency policies and procedures; (2) adequate notice of agency program information and decision-making processes; and (3) opportunities for commenting and providing information to agency staff.

Recent Developments

For nearly 20 years, the State of Indiana has made great strides in promoting environmental justice. And the state's contributions to the national EJ movement have not gone unnoticed. In 2002, the National Academy of Public Administration—a congressionally-charted non-partisan organization—published a report on the environmental justice efforts of four states, which identified Indiana as one of four "models for change."

While Indiana's early EJ contributions warrant praise, the state's program is not without deficiencies. IDEM's 2006 EJ policy, among other things, affirms the importance of meaningful public participation in the environmental decision-making process, emphasizes adequate public notice of agency activities through communications other than English, and seeks to broaden an "institutional awareness of differences in local conditions and population groups." Overall, however, the policy represents a general departure from the agency's initial focus on low-income, minority populations. Rather, as noted in the *PLRI Survey*, "it promotes the idea of participatory democracy by all affected populations."

Access to information—whether related to the environmental decision-making process, potential environmental hazards to local communities, or other matters—is a core principle of the EJ movement. Many of IDEM's early initiatives, such as the *Guide to Citizen Participation*, indicated the importance the agency placed on this principle in developing its EJ program. Recently, IDEM seems to have fallen short in prioritizing access to information. In particular, the *Guide* is currently unavailable. According to itswebsite, "IDEM is presently working on many updates to the document." However, "a timeline for completion of the new Guide for Citizen Participation has not be established." Another issue relates to the structure and organization of IDEM's website. While the site as a whole contains a variety of information on environmental education and how to protect your home and community, the agency's environmental justice webpage is severely limited in its resources, providing links only to IDEM's internal EJ policy and a handful of documents from the EPA and a single NGO.

Sources

Bullard, Robert D., ed. The Quest for Environmental Justice: Human Rights and the Politics of Pollution (2005).

Rechtschaffen, Clifford, Eileen Gauna & Catherine A. O'Neil, Environmental Justice: Law Policy & Regulation (2d ed. 2009).

Rhodes, Edwardo Lao. Environmental Justice in America: A New Paradigm (2003).

7

Environmental Racism Is Supported by the Evidence

H. Spencer Banzhaf

H. Spencer Banzhaf is Professor in the Dept. of Economics at Georgia State's Andrew Young School of Policy Studies.

There is indisputable evidence that environmental racism exists. Many factors exacerbate this. For example, poor people are attracted to lower-cost neighborhoods where pollution may exist. Moreover, firms may target non-white neighborhoods for polluting projects based on the belief that people of color lack access to institutional levers of power, and often vote less. A vicious spiral of injustice is the result. So how do we deal with it? H. Spencer Banzhaf suggests local participation, and bolstering the racially and economically disempowered overall.

Welcome to the RFF Weekly Policy Commentary, which is meant to provide an easy way to learn about important policy issues related to environmental, natural resource, energy, urban, and public health problems.

Poor people and minorities are more likely to live in neighborhoods at greater risk of environmental hazards. In this week's commentary, Spencer Banzhaf discusses to what extent, if any, public policy intervention might be warranted on the grounds

"The Political Economy of Environmental Justice," H. Spencer Banzhaf, Resources for the Future (RFF), May 25, 2009. Reproduced with the permission of Resources for the Future, www.rff.org.

of environmental justice and, if so, what form such interventions should take.

Over the years, the hard evidence, both documentary and academic, has shown convincingly that poor people and minorities are more likely than other groups to live in polluted neighborhoods. This pattern has been found again and again, in numerous places and with all sorts of pollutants. For example, disadvantaged groups live closer to hazardous waste facilities and landfills, live closer to large air polluters, and live in communities with higher measures of air pollution.

These findings have sparked the "environmental justice" movement, which has had mixed success in pushing its agenda. At the federal level, it won an important victory when President Clinton issued Executive Order 12898. Still in force, the order requires nondiscrimination in federal environmental programs and focuses federal resources on low-income and minority communities. However, the movement has failed to see an environmental justice act passed in Congress, though several have been introduced. It has also been rebuffed in its pursuit of legal action in federal courts under the Civil Rights Act. But other victories have come at the local level. Stakeholders have won a bigger voice in the approval process for new polluting facilities. And in one prominent case, local activists forced California's Southeast Air Quality Management District to settle a suit over the geographic distribution of pollution under its pollution trading program.

Sources of Environmental Inequity

But before prescribing any remedies for environmental inequity, it is essential that we understand the social mechanisms underlying it. Such mechanisms determine the nature and locus of any injustice, how a policy affects the distribution of pollution across places and population groups, and who bears the costs and who reaps the benefits of cleanups.

Consider just three of the most likely sources of the disproportionate pollution burden borne by disadvantaged groups.

First, disadvantaged groups have less political power. Consequently, they may be less successful at lobbying government agencies to block polluting facilities in their neighborhoods. Likewise, they may be less successful at pressuring such agencies to monitor existing facilities for compliance with environmental regulations. Closing the circle, polluting firms therefore may seek out such communities for the very reason that they know they will not be scrutinized so closely. There is some evidence for this mechanism, with pollution increasing in areas with lower voter turnout. If the correlation between pollution and demographics lies in these mechanisms, then it arises from government failures. In this case, either governmental reforms are required—or alternatively, nongovernmental mechanisms for determining pollution patterns should be considered.

Second, disadvantaged groups may live in more polluted areas for the simple reason that to be poor means not having the resources to "purchase" the good things in life—including a clean environment. By that I mean the ability to buy or rent a house or apartment in a clean neighborhood, which will be more expensive than one in a polluted neighborhood. The rich can afford to pay this premium while the poor cannot. In other words, firms may make their polluting decisions based on factors that have nothing whatsoever to do with local demographics, yet households will move in such a way that the poor end up living nearer pollution. In this case, the source of environmental inequity is the more fundamental inequity in the distribution of income.

But this mechanism has an important implication: the observed demographic patterns arise from decisions that individuals have made to make the best use of their limited resources. Saving money for food and clothing through inexpensive housing may be a higher priority for the poor than a clean environment. A cleanup may cause a neighborhood to gentrify, increasing housing prices. While this represents a capital gain to owners, 83 percent of people poor enough to qualify for welfare are renters. For them, these costs are out of their pocket, and can make the poor worse off in the end. In effect, the cleanup often forces the poor to pay a price they cannot afford.

A third and final mechanism may be that some communities have features that are attractive to both disadvantaged households and polluting firms. For example, both may be attracted to lower real estate prices. Moreover, real estate prices may be lower near transportation corridors like highways or railroads. The poor live near them because of these lower costs; polluting facilities may locate near them because the transportation route reduces the cost of moving manufactured goods or wastes. And finally, both poorer households and polluting facilities may be mutually attracted by low-skilled labor markets. In this case, the correlation between pollution and disadvantaged groups again arises from the simple fact that these groups have lower incomes. The effect is reinforced by the unhappy coincidence that some features of the inexpensive communities affordable for the poor are actually attractive to polluters.

Avoiding Unintended Consequences

For existing cleanup efforts such as the Superfund and brownfields programs, these mechanisms suggest guidelines that can help minimize unintended consequences like gentrification. Two recommendations stand out. First, as emphasized by the National Environmental Justice Advisory Council, projects should involve local participation. This will increase the likelihood that new amenities fit the preferences of incumbent residents rather than those of prospective gentrifiers. Second, projects might prioritize areas with high rates of home ownership, where local residents will capture the full value of the cleanup.

But there is a larger point at stake. When experiencing poor environmental quality is a consequence, rather than a cause, of poverty, then cleaning up the environment to help the poor is like treating the symptom rather than the disease. Some symptoms, like a moderate fever, represent the body's best efforts to heal itself. In such cases, treating the symptom may actually be counterproductive.

This does not mean there is no role for a physician. But the best physician facilitates the body's natural healing processes. Like the body, the market is a remarkably efficient machine.

Accordingly, the best way to help disadvantaged groups may be to empower them, strengthening their position within the market system. Redistributing income to the poor, for example, would provide them with more resources to pay for those things they most want, including a cleaner environment. Encouraging home ownership would put more people in a position to truly benefit from neighborhood improvements such as environmental cleanups. Providing legal aid, facilitating conflict resolution, and otherwise helping poor residents in environmental disputes can help the legal bargaining process to function better and enable the poor to participate in it fully. These may be the more effective routes for helping the poor—and prove to have "win, win" outcomes for society.

8

Economics Cannot Justify Unequal Environmental Risks

Rachel Massey

Rachel Massey is Senior Associate Director and Policy Program Manager at the Massachusetts Toxics Use Reduction Institute at the University of Massachusetts Lowell.

Economists use analytical tools to measure how environment harm affects different people unequally. For example, the concept of hedonic pricing described below assigns a value for the premium people pay to a live a neighborhood without pollution. These economic concepts become problematic when applied to the valuation of human life, since lower wages in poorer countries necessarily lower the value of a theoretical life. As economists deal with climate change and waste trade, they must guard against theories that justify further victimizing the powerless, as described in this excerpted article.

4. The Economics of Pollution and Health

The Theory of Externalities

What does economic analysis have to tell us about the problem of environmental justice? Standard environmental economic theory recognizes a concept—**externalities**—that is useful in understanding some of the important issues in this area. Externalities arise when a market transaction affects individuals or firms other than those involved in the transaction. A negative

"Environmental Justice: Income, Race, and Health. Types of environmental racism," by Rachel Massey, Tufts University. Reprinted by permission.

externality arises when a market transaction imposes *costs* on individuals or firms not involved in the transaction; a positive externality arises when those individuals or firms enjoy a *benefit* from the transaction.

From an environmental justice perspective, we can see an additional dimension to the problem of externalities: in many cases, the principal bearers of negative externalities are the poor and underprivileged. For example, distant stockholders may profit from operation of a polluting factory, while people living next to the factory become ill or die from the effects of the pollution.

Efficiency and Equity

Economists define **efficiency** in terms of total welfare gains and losses. An efficient policy is one that maximizes total net welfare gains for society as a whole. **Equity**, in contrast, is defined on the basis of *who* gains or loses. A policy that is efficient is not necessarily equitable, and may in fact be rejected on an equity basis. For example, a policy that makes a rich person $1,000 richer while a poor person grows $800 poorer is "economically efficient," because it offers a net social gain of $200. Such a policy is not equitable, however, because it benefits the wealthy at the expense of the poor. In many cases, as we have seen in the discussion above, distribution of environmental harms is not equitable. Society's pursuit of efficiency may lead to greater overall wealth, while the negative environmental externalities accompanying economic growth fall mainly on lower-income people.

Hedonic Pricing

Economists sometimes examine the relationship between pollution and location through the study of **hedonic pricing**. Hedonic pricing attempts to calculate the dollar value of environmental factors by looking at variations in the value of marketed goods, such as houses or land. For example, economists may compare property values between two neighborhoods that are largely similar in terms of home size, access to schools, and other factors. If one neighborhood contains a toxic waste site and the other is relatively unpolluted, the more polluted neighborhood is likely to have lower property values. By isolating the effect of the toxic waste site on property values, economists estimate the implicit dollar value people place on being protected from pollution. Many studies have found that as pollution increases, property values go down. Of course, this principle implies that those who can best afford to pay to avoid pollution will be able to escape negative impacts of toxic wastes.

Valuing Human Life and Health

In some uses of economic analysis, income differences can be presented as a justification for unequal distribution of environmental harms. This approach can be particularly problematic when it relies on monetary values assigned to human lives.

When an economic activity poses threats to human health or human lives, economists may undertake to discuss the "value of a human life." While one might reasonably feel that this value is inestimable, when policy decisions regarding pollution prevention are involved, the question often arises of how much it is worth spending per estimated life saved. One approach is to calculate the **value of a statistical life**. Methodologies for calculating the value of a "statistical life" include so-called wage-risk analyses and analyses of foregone future income.

In wage-risk analyses, economists collect data and perform calculations to find out how much money people are generally willing to spend in order to avoid a small risk of death. For example, they may look at the wage premium associated with working in a dangerous job, and extrapolate to estimate the value of a person's life. Analyses of foregone future income look at the amount a person would have earned over the remainder of his or her lifetime, if he or she had survived. This approach puts a higher value on people who were likely to become rich than on people who were expected to pursue a middle- or low-income career path.

Compensation and Relocation

One approach to dealing with equity in economic analysis is the principle of **compensation**. If one group of people suffers from a particular economic activity or policy, they can—in theory—be compensated for their loss. In practice, however, those who suffer from environmental pollution rarely receive adequate compensation. Indeed, it is not clear that any level of compensation is adequate when health damages are very severe.

In 1980, families in Love Canal, a community near Niagara Falls in New York State, succeeded in pressuring the Federal government to relocate them off the contaminated land where they had purchased homes and were raising children. The families in Love Canal had not been informed when they purchased their homes that Hooker Chemical, a local company, had buried tons of hazardous waste in the neighborhood before the homes were built. Highly toxic wastes were seeping into these families' homes and the school playground, causing severe illnesses in local children. Love Canal families had, in many cases, put all their savings into purchasing homes in what they thought was a safe, desirable neighborhood for their children to grow up in. In 1978, when they discovered the truth about the toxic pollution in their backyards, basements, and schoolyard, they lacked the resources to simply abandon the homes they had purchased and relocate.

After years of struggle, these families won an agreement with the Federal government in which they were given the resources to move to safer neighborhoods. Decades later, however, many other communities across the U.S. face similar situations. In many of these cases, the communities that are now fighting for relocation were there long before the industrial facilities that are driving them away. For example, the Diamond community of Norco, Louisiana, has fought for relocation for decades.[24] Diamond is a primarily black community; many residents own their homes, and many families have lived on the same land for generations. In the 1950s, Shell Corporation built a chemical facility directly adjacent to the community; the plant's fence line is 25 feet from people's homes. The community is flanked on the other side by a refinery.

Residents of Diamond suffer regularly from respiratory problems, headaches, and a variety of other symptoms. A 1997 health survey found that over a third of the children in the community had asthma. A quarter of the women and children in the community had been treated in an emergency room at some point due to respiratory problems. Air samples collected by a community group found extremely high levels of cancer-causing chemicals in the air. When a Shell accident killed two residents in 1973, Shell spent a total of $3,500 to make amends: $3,000 to purchase the home of one victim, and $500 in compensation to the other victim's mother. In June 2002, after years of negotiation, the community reached a relocation agreement with Shell.

The economic methodology of human life valuation can also be the basis for concluding that the lives of people in wealthy countries are worth more than the lives of similar people in developing countries, where average pay is lower. This view was notoriously expressed in a 1991 memo by Lawrence Summers, then president of the World Bank, in which he suggested that the World Bank should encourage migration of highly polluting industries to poor countries. Summers' memo suggested that the World Bank should be *encouraging* migration of "dirty industries" to poor countries. His reasoning included the following:

> The measurements of the costs of health impairing pollution depends on the foregone earnings from increased morbidity and mortality. From this point of view a given amount of health impairing pollution should be done in the country with the lowest cost, which will be the country with the lowest wages. I think the economic logic behind dumping a load of toxic waste in the lowest wage country is impeccable and we should face up to that.[25]

Summers later said that he was not serious about this argument; he meant it simply as an exploration of where economic logic could lead. Whether or not Summers was serious about this argument, logic of this kind is incorporated into many economic analyses of environmental policy options. In 1995, economists analyzing the impacts of climate change for the Intergovernmental Panel on Climate Change (IPCC) valued lives of citizens of rich countries at $1.5 million, in middle-income countries at $300,000, and in low-income countries at $100,000.[26] This led to a major political backlash from outraged citizens of developing nations. Later IPCC reports recommended a possible compromise value of $1 million for the value of a life regardless of country of residence. Clearly, the issue of valuing human life will remain highly controversial whatever methodology is adopted.

5. International Dimensions of Environmental Justice

Just as poor communities often bear a disproportionate burden of pollution and environmental degradation compared with wealthier communities within the same country, poor nations may bear a disproportionate burden from toxic wastes that are exported from wealthier nations. Poor nations may also bear a disproportionate burden from **global warming** and other human-induced changes that affect the entire planet.

Global warming is an example of problems both of environmental externalities and of equity issues on a planetary scale. The "greenhouse effect" is a process in which gases such as carbon dioxide build up in the earth's atmosphere and trap energy from the sun. Factories, cars, airplanes, and other mainstays of industrialized living all increase the levels of carbon dioxide and other greenhouse gases into the atmosphere. Through the greenhouse effect, these gases contribute to global warming.

The Intergovernmental Panel on Climate Change (IPCC), an international body of scientists, has developed a series of scenarios from which predictions can be made about likely changes associated with global warming.[27] Expected changes include higher temperatures in many parts of the world, greater likelihood of droughts and flooding, increased frequency and severity of storms, and rising sea level.[28]

International negotiations are under way to allocate responsibility for bringing global warming under control before it is too late. In these negotiations, the U.S. and other developed countries have pushed to ensure that developing countries also bear some of the burden of reducing global emissions of greenhouse gases. At the same time, there is widespread recognition that the gains and losses have not been fairly distributed. Developed countries have enjoyed most of the gains from rapid industrial expansion and widespread use of automobiles and other fuel-intensive forms of transportation. Developing countries, on the other hand, are predicted to bear the most serious consequences from global warming.

Unequal Burden from Global Warming

Bangladesh is a densely populated country of some 115 million people, living in an area of about 144,000 square kilometers. Bangladesh is located at the delta of three major rivers, and is subject to severe flooding. Some scholars have looked at the likely effects of a one-meter sea level rise in Bangladesh. According to one study, if sea level rises by a meter, over 11% of the population of Bangladesh (over 13 million people) will be displaced; nearly a fifth of the total land area of the country will be completely flooded; and unique mangrove forests will be lost. In addition, more than a fifth of the country's monsoon rice land will be covered with water, and coastal shrimp production will become impossible (See maps showing areas of Bangladesh likely to be inundated under "low" and "high" sea-level rise projections).

One possible option for combating the effects of a sea-level of this magnitude may be to build barriers, or dykes, to protect areas in Bangladesh. This measure would only address the one problem of sea level rise, and would not deal with the mild problem that global warming is likely to increase the frequency and severity of cyclones and other destructive weather

The likely effects of global warming in Bangladesh exemplify the unequal burden of environmental problems that result from some economic activities. The contribution of Bangladesh itself to global warming is minimal; yet Bangladesh will bear some of the greatest costs of rising temperatures on earth.

International Trade in Toxics

Nobody wants hazardous waste, but hazardous waste is traded internationally just like desirable goods, such as food and clothing. Many people believe that international trade in hazardous waste places an unfair burden on the countries that receive it. The option to send hazardous waste abroad also makes it easier for firms in wealthy countries to keep producing the waste, because they do not have to find room for it within their own communities. An international treaty, the **Basel Convention,** was created in 1989 to place limits on international trade in toxic wastes.

In 1994, signatories to the Basel Convention agreed on a total ban on exports of hazardous wastes from developed to less developed countries. The 15 countries of the European Union have implemented the Basel Convention and banned the export of all hazardous wastes to developing countries for any reason. To date, the U.S. is the only developed country that has not ratified the Basel Convention.

Exporting Toxics—The Case of Guiyu

An investigation conducted in 2001 by the Basel Action Network, a non-governmental organization, documented highly hazardous practices in one rural area of China where electronic equipment is dismantled to recover valuable components. Around 100,000 people work in the electronics "recycling" operations of Guiyu, many of them women and children.

Electronic equipment is dismantled by hand using simple tools such as hammers and screwdrivers. Minimal or no precautions exist to protect workers from the toxic substances contained in the equipment. For example, workers dismantling used toner cartridges use paintbrushes and their bare hands to remove remaining toner; they breathe the toner dust and it covers their clothing. Printer toners contain a substance known as carbon black, a likely human carcinogen.

Other workers burn plastic-coated wires to recover the valuable copper within them. The polyvinyl chloride (PVC) coating of the wires, as well as brominated flame retardants in the wire insulation, are likely to produce the highly toxic chemicals known as dioxins and furans when they burn. Children and pregnant women live close to the burning operations, and small children play in the toxic ashes. A near-by fishpond, which is likely to be contaminated by the burning byproducts, is a major source of nutrition for the village. Glass from computer and television monitors, which contains large amounts of lead, is dumped in rivers or on open land.

At the time of this study, electronic waste "recycling" had been carried out in Guiyu for the past six years. For five of those years, drinking water has had to be trucked into the area, because all the local water sources are too contaminated to drink.

The Problem of Electronics Waste

Computers and other electronic equipment contain large amounts of heavy metals and other toxic substances. For example, a typical cathode ray tube (CRT) computer monitor contains three to eight pounds of lead. Lead is hazardous to the nervous system, blood, kidneys, and reproductive systems, and causes irreversible brain damage in children. Millions of pounds of toxic electronic waste, or "E-waste," are generated each year within the U.S. alone, as we discard outdated computers, televisions, and other obsolete equipment. [30]

With increasing knowledge about the hazards associated with these wastes, some communities within the U.S. have taken steps to protect themselves. Massachusetts and California, for example, have laws against disposing of cathode ray tube monitors—the monitors used for most personal computers and television screens—in municipal landfills.[31] But when toxic electronic waste of this kind is diverted from landfills in the U.S., it is often exported overseas. An estimated 50% to 80% of the televisions and computer monitors that U.S. consumers bring to recycling centers are actually exported to poor communities in Asia.

Once in Asia, this electronic equipment is not recycled in the way we might imagine. Some of the materials are recovered for further use, but the way the materials are extracted poses tragically severe health consequences for the people doing the work and for their families and neighbors. In China, India, and Pakistan, electronics "recycling" is associated with hazardous activities including open burning of plastics, which can produce highly toxic byproducts; exposure to toxic solders; and dumping of acids in rivers. Many of the workers who are exposed to these hazardous byproducts are children.

The case of trade in toxic e-waste reveals a paradox of the economic success of the computer industry. Part of the enormous growth in the computer and electronics industry has been linked to rapid obsolescence of equipment. Whereas electronic equipment was once considered a long-term investment, much of it is now designed to be thrown away after several years. According to a 1999 report by the National Safety Council, the average life span of a computer in the U.S. is now as low as two years.[32]

The flow of hazardous "e-waste" to Asia results in part from low wages in Asia and lax or poorly enforced regulations to protect workers' health. In addition, it is legal in the U.S. to export hazardous waste, despite international laws to the contrary.

The problem of hazardous e-waste also results from the way in which these products are designed. For the most part, electronics are not designed to facilitate recycling. Thus, the recycling that does occur is labor intensive and hazardous, and many materials are wasted because they cannot be recovered from the products.

The solution to the problem of hazardous e-waste lies at least partly in pursuing clean production. If electronic equipment is designed to be easily and efficiently recycled, resources can be saved while workers' health is protected. New legislation on electronics in the European Union makes manufacturers responsible for eliminating some of the most toxic components of electronic equipment, and creates incentives or requirements for manufacturers to create easily recycled products.

[…]

7. Summary

Environmental justice is the recognition that minority and low-income communities often bear a disproportionate share of environmental costs—and the perception that this is unjust. Environmental quality, income levels, and access to health care can all affect people's health. People with low incomes and inadequate access to health care are often disproportionately exposed to environmental contamination that threatens their health. Environmental pollution is linked to a range of disabilities and chronic illnesses including cancer, asthma, and certain learning disabilities. Rising rates of these problems affect everyone, but in many cases, poor and minority communities are disproportionately affected.

Across the United States, poor and minority neighborhoods bear an unequal burden from hazardous facilities and waste sites. Pollution is also distributed unequally within individual states, within counties, and within cities. Hazardous waste sites, municipal landfills, incinerators, and other hazardous facilities are disproportionately located in poor and minority neighborhoods.

A variety of economic concepts are relevant to the study of the interrelationship among income, pollution, and health. For example, economists sometimes examine the relationship between pollution and location through the study of hedonic pricing. Hedonic pricing attempts to calculate the dollar value of environmental factors by looking at variations in the value of marketed goods, such as houses or land.

The difference between efficiency and equity is also important for an understanding of the economics of pollution and health. Economists define efficiency in terms of total welfare gains and losses. Equity, in contrast, is defined on the basis of who gains or loses. A policy that is efficient is not necessarily equitable, and may in fact be rejected on an equity basis. In many cases, distribution of environmental harms is not equitable. Externalities arise when a market transaction affects individuals or firms other than those involved in the transaction. A negative externality arises when a market transaction imposes costs on individuals or firms not involved in the transaction; a positive externality arises when those individuals or firms enjoy a benefit from the transaction.

In some uses of economic analysis, income differences can be presented as a justification for unequal distribution of environmental harms. This approach can be particularly problematic when it relies on defining the monetary value of a human life. Methodologies for calculating the value of a "statistical life" include so-called wage-risk analyses and analyses of foregone future income.

Just as poor communities often bear a disproportionate burden of pollution and environmental degradation compared with wealthier communities within the same country, poor nations may bear a disproportionate burden from toxic wastes that are exported from wealthier nations. Poor nations may also bear a disproportionate burden from global warming and other human-induced changes that affect the entire planet. For example, global warming is caused by fossil fuel use, which historically has been concentrated in developed countries; yet the adverse effects of global warming may be concentrated disproportionately in certain developing countries.

References

23 National Institutes of Health Data Fact Sheet: Asthma Statistics, January 1999. Data are drawn from the National Center for Health Statistics, Vital Statistics of the United States.

24 Information on Norco is drawn from http://www.labucketbrigade.org/communities /norco/profile/index.shtml, viewed October 2004.

25 Lawrence Summers, World Bank, internal memo, December 12, 1991. Reproduced at: http://www.sustainableworld.org.uk/summersmemo.htm.

26 Ackerman and Heinzerling (2004), *Priceless: On Knowing the Price of Everything and the Value of Nothing*, pp. 73–4.

27 See http://www.grida.no/climate/ipcc_tar

28 For a summary, see Summary for Policymakers: A Report of Working Group 1 of the Intergovernmental Panel on Climate Change, available at http://www.grida.no/climate

/ipcc_tar/vol4/english/pdf/wg1spm.pdf and IPCC, Climate Change 2001: Synthesis Report [Watson, R.T. and the Core Writing Team (eds.)]. (New York: Cambridge University Press, 2001) at http://www.grida.no/climate/ipcc_tar/vol4/english/index.htm

29 See Saleemul Huq (1999), *Vulnerability and Adaptation to Climate Change for Bangladesh* (Boston: Kluwer Academic Publishers).

30 Unless otherwise noted, information on this electronics waste is taken from Puckett et al. (2002), *Exporting Harm: The High-Tech Trashing of Asia.*

31 Puckett et al. (2002), p. 4.

32 National Safety Council (1999), Electronic Product Recovery and Recycling Baseline Report, cited in Puckett et al (2002).

9

"Environmental Justice" Obscures Persistent Racism

Bryan K. Bullock

Bryan K. Bullock is a civil rights attorney and community activist in Gary, Indiana. He was formerly habeas counsel for detainees in Guantanamo Bay.

Environmental racism is not the same as environmental justice. In fact, the latter term may constitute an erasure of the paramount issue of racism. People of color still must deal with far more threats to their health, and also face major impediments to community self-determination. The use of euphemistic terms like "diversity" and "inclusion" obscure this central and tenacious problem, according to the viewpoint below.

The movement against environmental racism lost its way when it was subsumed into environmental "justice." Racism remains paramount. "African descendant people are burdened by environmental issues unequally compared to their white counterparts." The struggle demands a human rights approach. "We must recognize that although we are separated by land, sea and language, we are united in our desire to reclaim and maintain our basic humanity."

"Reviving the Fight Against Environmental Racism, Bryan K. Bullock, Black Agenda Report, November 3, 2015. Reprinted by permission.

"White environmentalists talk about saving the rainforests, but no mention is ever made of saving the lives of those who dwell in America's concrete jungles."

It's time to get back to basics in the struggle for true freedom for African Americans. The "basics" in this sense, means reclaiming strategies that were identified in the heady days of the 60's and 70's, that seem to have fallen out of vogue, while the issues that the strategies of that era were created to address, remain to this day. Basic strategies like community control of the police as well as community control over the institutions and resources in black communities, are being heard again by a new generation of activists. Getting back to basics also includes re-claiming the word *racism*. Politicians, academics and activists have allowed the raw power of the word *racism* to be euphemized into words like *justice, diversity, inclusion,* and *equity,* to name a few.

Nowhere is this seen more clearly than in the issue of environmental racism. Black environmental activists were fighting against the placing of landfills, toxic waste dumps, abandoned buildings, lead paint, and Superfund sites in their communities, because these issues were specifically affecting them in the spaces and places where they live and because white environmental activists were not coming to their rescue. Nothing has changed in that regard. What has changed is that instead of talking about environmental racism, black activists use the word environmental justice. However, racism is still the issue.

Environmental racism was either high-jacked or subsumed into environmental justice, depending on one's viewpoint, to recognize that poor people, regardless of race, face environmental issues in their communities. However, the overwhelming number of poor people who must deal with sprawl, abandoned buildings, and brownfields, food deserts, lack of transportation (which results in the use of more cars), landfills, and polluted air are still overwhelmingly black and brown. Environmental justice language talks about benefits and burdens. But African descendant people are burdened by environmental issues unequally compared to their white counterparts. To the extent that poor whites face similar environmental concerns, they have a major benefit, namely that they are often helped by the local Sierra Club, Natural Resources Defense Council, or some other local white environmental organization. Black communities don't get the same kind of attention from white environmentalists. Additionally white environmental organizations often get grants from the Environmental Protection Agency (EPA) or some other government agency to do "environmental justice" projects. But those grant resources rarely benefit black people. And since there are no Sierra Clubs in the hood, white environmentalists don't live in the communities that are the focus of the environmental justice grants and so they don't even know what issues exists in these populations. White environmentalists are purposely or naively blind to the racism that is still entrenched within their organizations and therefore can't see the racism behind the environmental issues in black communities.

"Environmental racism was either high-jacked or subsumed into environmental justice."

This is why they do not focus their efforts on the special environmental concerns of people of color. They are basically concerned about preserving pristine wild areas, but not about poverty stricken urban areas. White environmentalists talk about saving the rainforests, but no mention is ever made of saving the lives of those who dwell in America's concrete jungles. When they talk of clean air and clean water they rarely seem to apply that concern to those who live in majority black cities where factories, landfills, and waste incinerators are located. The hole in the ozone layer and global warming, although very important topics, never seem to have black victims who need help to escape from rising temperatures. There is great talk of saving endangered species, like white polar bears, yet not many environmentalists ever discuss saving young black men who many also consider to be an endangered species.

New organizations and coalitions spring up to take the issue of environmental justice, yet few deal with environmental racism. The Moral Monday Movement has working groups to address environmental justice, yet environmental racism is not on the agenda. They talk about issues like net metering and solar panels, none of which specifically address the needs of poor black people. The white environmental justice advocates in the Moral Monday Movement are rarely concerned with racism and the specific environmental issues facing black populations. They, like other majority-led working groups and organizations, live in a white world where what's good for the suburbs and the rainforests are good for everyone. They can't fathom the fact black and brown people have particular environmental issues that are outside of their limited perspective. The result is that environmentalism is just as segregated today as it was 20 years ago.

This is why African Americans have to develop their own environmental organizations if the specific environmental issues facing African descendant people are to be dealt with. Food deserts, brownfields, toxic waste sites, landfills, transportation issues, abandoned gas stations, all affect black people in particular ways. These are issues of racism, not esoteric, pliable words like justice. All of the myriad of issues faced by black people, are the result of racism. As the Kerner Commission stated, black communities are created and maintained by racism. This is no less true when it comes to the environment in those black communities. Black activists must reclaim environmental racism and leave environmental justice to those white or multi-racial configurations that want to help them fight them racism.

"Environmentalism is just as segregated today as it was 20 years ago."

As usual, black people cannot expect for the EPA (or the government in general), the Sierra Club, the Natural Resources Defense Council, Greenpeace, or any other white environmental organization to address the specific needs in our communities. The NAACP has finally begun to address environmental justice (racism) in its plank of concerns, but more importantly, black and brown grassroots organizations around the country have sprung up to fight for the right to have a clean environment in their communities. Even mult-racial outfits like Moral Mondays are inadequate to the task. Black environmentalists, like the black protestors in Ferguson, must lead the charge in their own spaces and places, and white supporters will then jump on board. Ultimately, this is nothing new. It simply speaks to what happens when black people lose sight of the specifics of African experience in America and let ourselves and our issues get co-opted by better funded, less radical, reformist majority white formations like the environmental movement. Getting back to basics simply means accepting the reality of racism in America and in environmentalism, and leading our movements to address our own issues.

The environmental justice movement may be the most important civil rights issue of the 21st century. It bridges the gap between environmental concerns, civil rights and human rights. The Civil Rights Movement brought wide, sweeping change to the American landscape. Activists, attorneys and academics banded together to fight against the forces that had been allied against them, forces that waged war on their very humanity. The war to oppress people of color is an ongoing, never-ending war, as evidenced in the continuing issues of employment discrimination, police brutality, poor educational opportunities and the portrayal of the black as the criminal, coon, vixen and savage in popular culture. Landfills and hazardous waste facilities continue to be disproportionately sited in communities of color. The assault on the humanity of African-Americans and the indigenous people of America threatens their health as well as the viability of the places and spaces where they reside. The assault on the environment and human rights continues in Palestine, as the state-less, impoverished and out-gunned face unfettered harassment, destruction and death even as their lands are appropriated, occupied and destroyed. Black and brown and poor people in Gary, Indiana, find commonality in their lives with the black, brown and poor people in far flung places like the Philippines, Brazil, Nigeria, Palestine, and Iraq. Yet these are commonalities that are linked by human rights and not civil rights.

"Black environmentalists, like the black protestors in Ferguson, must lead the charge in their own spaces and places."

Poor people and people of color around the globe are threatened by economic insecurity, poverty, disenfranchisement, disinvestment, disinterest, under-education, and environmental degradation. These are, in the final analysis, human problems. The food famine in Africa may be credibly linked to the famine of new and progressive black leadership due to the lack of cultivation of the fertile soil of black minds. When the colonial powers were forced to leave Asian and African lands, they divested their riches from these countries, yet they continued to make money off of the backs of the formerly oppressed. When the colonial powers left the inner city, they divested their riches, yet they continue to make money off the backs of the people still trapped there. Although the civil rights struggle challenged the myriad of social inequities facing African Americans in particular, and other people of color and poor whites as well, it has not proved to be a deterrent to the continued war against people of color and the poor.

The environmental justice movement, like other civil rights movements, has rooted its struggle in the text of American laws. Environmental justice movement members too are beginning to see that American laws, while useful and necessary, are subject to the whims of racist judges, cowardly law-makers and ambivalent law-enforcers. But the unique thing about the environmental justice movement is that the battle to live in a clean environment is one that people around the world are fighting. Human rights may hold the answer to the environmental justice movement in a way that civil rights may not. The US Constitution does not explicitly guarantee its citizens the right to a clean environment. However, the Universal Declaration on Human Rights does. Law makers and judges in America have not linked the ability of Americans to exercise their rights under the Constitution to their need for breathable air, drinkable water and unpolluted soil. Civil rights have guaranteed people of color the ability to purchase homes that they can afford. But what good is that right when one has no right not to have a landfill or a toxic waste dump located near their new home? What good does it do a person to have the right to speak freely, when they have no right to breathe clean air?

"Human rights may hold the answer to the environmental justice movement in a way that civil rights may not."

Although the right to freedom from discrimination is a civil right guaranteed by US law, its importance is strengthened by its status as a human right. People have civil rights because they are people. Human rights exist independently of the Constitution and independently of the state; they carry not only legal weight, but moral weight as well. Environmental justice provides a perfect nexus between human rights and the environment. Environmental human rights, as defined by several United Nations Declarations, include civil, cultural, economic, political and social rights, as does the concept of environmental justice. The prevailing view among US politicians is that human rights are for other countries, civil rights are for us. Practically speaking, civil rights are granted by governments; human rights exist by the fact of one being born and cannot be taken by away by governments. Civil rights may vary from nation to nation, but human rights are universal. They are as universal, natural and God-given as air, land, water, and soil.

Human rights exist because the Creator created humans and the environmental justice movement exists for the same reason. Governments cannot create air, water, and soil, just as they cannot create humanity. Thus, environmental justice and human rights are linked in a way that lends itself to a new framework of discussion of rights and responsibilities. The laws of the US seem to contemplate, recognize, and accept the fact that it is socially, culturally, and legally acceptable to protect the health of some people, while knowingly placing other humans at risk. However, the Draft Declaration of Principles on Human Rights and the Environment explicitly addresses the rights of people to live in an environment of clean air and water. It also includes procedural rights such as the right of people to information affecting their environment, freedom of opinion and expression to speak freely about environmental issues, education, and the right to effective remedies. The declaration, most importantly, deals with duties. In particular, the duties that governments, transnational corporations and other international and national organizations have to prevent environmental degradation. The third principle of the Draft Declaration of Principles on Human Rights and the Environment states: "All persons shall be free from any form of discrimination in regard to actions and decisions that affect the environment." Whereas the federal government's Executive Order 12898 talks in terms of benefits and burdens, the Draft Declaration speaks a message of rights and responsibilities. Where the federal law requires federal, state, and local governments to countenance disproportionate impacts, international law requires remedial action against discrimination. Governments and their subdivisions may not initiate discriminatory activities or policies, nor may they tolerate them. Under international law, they have an affirmative obligation to eliminate existing discrimination.

"The Draft Declaration of Principles on Human Rights and the Environment explicitly addresses the rights of people to live in an environment of clean air and water."

Environmental injustice links the struggles of people of color and poor people around the world in real and tangible ways. The rich and powerful are linked by their ruthless attempts to maintain the status quo. The poor and marginalized are linked by their desperate need to overturn balances of power that are tilted perversely against them. The environment stretches from the ghettoes of New York and Chicago, to the impoverished communities of Gary and East Chicago, to the war torn streets of Baghdad. The people in East Chicago, Indiana, and the people in Soweto, South Africa, both are fighting governments and corporations in an effort to live in communities that are free of toxic pollutants. Citizens of Gary, Indiana, and La[g]os, Nigeria, are pawns, victims, and beneficiaries of industries that pollute their environment, influence their lawmakers and yet provide needed jobs. The industrialized nations of the world have produced great prosperity and great industrial waste. The citizens of East Chicago and Gary have benefited from the steel mills in their communities and they have been burdened by polluted air, contaminated water, and hopelessly polluted soil.

Poor people and people of color continue to have to fight for information and disclosure from governments and corporations regarding the environmental hazards and health effects of these hazards. Indeed, the inability to have a voice in the decision-making process leads to further isolation, marginalization, and victimization of the poor and people of color. The Global Consultation on the Right to Development as a Human Right states: Development strategies which have been oriented merely towards economic growth and financial considerations have failed to a large extent to achieve social justice; human rights have been infringed, directly and through the depersonalization of social relations, the breakdown of families and communities, of social and economic life.

"War is the greatest environmental hazard and the greatest threat to humanity ever created."

One of the greatest threats to the environment and to democracy, are the secret and undemocratic meetings of international bodies like the G20 and so-called free trade agreements. If a particular environmental regulation is deemed to be restrictive of trade, the US may be forced to repeal the law in the name of international trade. These are human rights and environmental justice concerns. As one author has written, "Examination of the socio-cultural context of environmental degradation leads to the clear conclusion that, in spite of international and national structures establishing inalienable rights for all people, some people experience greater harm than others, and in many cases this differential experience is a result of government-induced and/or government-sanctioned action." In the context of both human rights and environmental justice, the "some people" the author mentions are overwhelmingly people of color.

War is the greatest environmental hazard and the greatest threat to humanity ever created. Black and brown people from poor communities like Gary and Detroit, are shipped off to foreign lands to fight other poor black and brown people. In the process, they detonate mega-ton bombs, destroying the physical environment, killing people, and forever severing the bonds of humanity. Uranium-tipped ordnance contaminates the physical environment and the bodies of its victims. The indiscriminate bulldozing of homes in the West Bank and Gaza wreak havoc on the physical infrastructure of an entire society. In the parlance of the environmental justice movement, when one speaks of benefits and burdens, it must be understood that no one benefits from hatred and war.

All countries that have nuclear power produce nuclear waste. And all too often, it is the most vulnerable people in their respective nations who store the most waste in their backyards, in their skins and bones, and in the genes of their children. We face the greatest environmental hazard the world has ever seen in the proliferation and use of nuclear weapons. Devices that, once detonated, have the capacity to alter weather patterns, contaminate soil and air for generations, and destroy the natural and human ecology beyond recognition threaten the very survival of the planet we live on. If the link between environmental justice and human rights cannot be made within the context of war, then no linkage is possible.

"We face the greatest environmental hazard the world has ever seen in the proliferation and use of nuclear weapons."

Community activists in urban areas must link their struggles with community activists around the world. Local environmental justice activists must understand that Palestinians, Iraqis, Nigerians, and Burmese face the same problems of poverty, discrimination, and marginalization. Just as Malcolm X and W.E.B. DuBois recognized that the struggles of Patrice Lumuumba, Jomo Kenyatta, and Cesar Chavez were similar to their own struggles, environmental justice activists of today must relate their struggles to activists in faraway lands. We must recognize that although we are separated by land, sea, and language, we are united in our desire to reclaim and maintain our basic humanity. The environmental justice movement holds the potential for human rights activists to see the similarities of their problems, the similarities in the tactics of their oppressors and the similarities in the solutions. When that day comes, the oppressed people of the world, regardless of race, color, or religion, will speak with one unifying voice, saying "No more" to those who seek to locate toxic waste facilities, landfills, and medical wastes in our communities. As Malcolm X stated, when we begin to see ourselves as a majority that can demand, instead of a minority that must beg, we can literally move the world toward a just, sustainable, clean, multi-racial and respectful new world order.

10

Environmental Racism Does Not Exist

David Friedman

David Friedman is a writer, an international consultant, and fellow in the MIT Japan program.

This minority viewpoint claims that environmental racism is not a valid concern and has no basis in fact. The author claims that the foundational studies upon which the movement gained theoretical justification were flawed, and not even peer-reviewed. Friedman claims that the Clinton Administration used an Executive Order and bureaucracy to circumvent the lack of a political mandate for their mission to redress an environmental racism that others claim was overblown.

When the U.S. Environmental Protection Agency (EPA) unveiled its heavily criticized environmental justice "guidance" earlier this year, it crowned years of maneuvering to redress an "outrage" that doesn't exist. The agency claims that state and local policies deliberately cluster hazardous economic activities in politically powerless "communities of color." The reality is that the EPA, by exploiting every possible legal ambiguity, skillfully limiting debate, and ignoring even its own science, has enshrined some of the worst excesses of racialist rhetoric and environmental advocacy into federal law.

"The 'Environmental Racism' Hoax," David Friedman, *American Enterprise Institute for Public Policy Research*, 1998. Reprinted with the permission of the American Enterprise Institute.

"Environmental justice" entered the activist playbook after a failed 1982 effort to block a hazardous-waste landfill in a predominantly black North Carolina county. One of the protesters was the District of Columbia's congressional representative, who returned to Washington and prodded the General Accounting Office (GAO) to investigate whether noxious environmental risks were disproportionately sited in minority communities.

A year later, the GAO said that they were. Superfund and similar toxic dumps, it appeared, were disproportionately located in non-white neighborhoods. The well-heeled, overwhelmingly white environmentalist lobby christened this alleged phenomenon "environmental racism," and ethnic advocates like Ben Chavis and Robert Bullard built a grievance over the next decade.

Few of the relevant studies were peer-reviewed; all made critical errors. Properly analyzed, the data revealed that waste sites are just as likely to be located in white neighborhoods, or in areas where minorities moved only after permits were granted. Despite sensational charges of racial "genocide" in industrial districts and ghastly "cancer alleys," health data don't show minorities being poisoned by toxic sites. "Though activists have a hard time accepting it," notes Brookings fellow Christopher H. Foreman, Jr., a self-described black liberal Democrat, "racism simply doesn't appear to be a significant factor in our national environmental decision-making."

This reality, and the fact that the most ethnically diverse urban regions were desperately trying to attract employers, not sue them, constrained the environmental racism movement for a while. In 1992, a Democrat-controlled Congress ignored environmental justice legislation introduced by then-Senator Al Gore. Toxic racism made headlines, but not policy.

All of that changed with the Clinton-Gore victory. Vice President Gore got his former staffer Carol Browner appointed head of the EPA and brought Chavis, Bullard, and other activists into the transition government. The administration touted environmental justice as one of the symbols of its new approach.

Even so, it faced enormous political and legal hurdles. Legislative options, never promising in the first place, evaporated with the 1994 Republican takeover in Congress. Supreme Court decisions did not favor the movement.

So the Clinton administration decided to bypass the legislative and judicial branches entirely. In 1994, it issued an executive order—ironically cast as part of Gore's "reinventing government" initiative to streamline bureaucracy—which directed that every federal agency "make achieving environmental justice part of its mission."

At the same time, executive branch lawyers generated a spate of legal memoranda that ingeniously used a poorly defined section of the Civil Rights Act of 1964 as authority for environmental justice programs. Badly split, confusing Supreme Court decisions seemed to construe the 1964 Act's "nondiscrimination" clause (prohibiting federal funds for states that discriminate racially) in such a way as to allow federal intervention wherever a state policy ended up having "disparate effects" on different ethnic groups.

Even better for the activists, the Civil Rights Act was said to authorize private civil rights lawsuits against state and local officials on the basis of disparate impacts. This was a valuable tool for environmental and race activists, who are experienced at using litigation to achieve their ends.

Its legal game plan in place, the EPA then convened an advocate-laden National Environmental Justice Advisory Council (NEJAC), and seeded activist groups (to the tune of $3 million in 1995 alone) to promote its policies. Its efforts paid off. From 1993, the agency backlogged over 50 complaints, and environmental justice rhetoric seeped into state and federal land-use decisions.

Congress, industry, and state and local officials were largely unaware of these developments because, as subsequent news reports and congressional hearings established, they were deliberately excluded from much of the agency's planning process. Contrary perspectives, including EPA-commissioned studies highly critical of the research cited by the agency to justify its environmental justice initiative in the first place, were ignored or suppressed.

The EPA began to address a wider audience in September 1997. It issued an "interim final guidance" (bureaucratese for regulation-like rules that agencies can claim are not "final" so as to avoid legal challenge) which mandated that environmental justice be incorporated into all projects that file federal environmental impact statements. The guidance directed that applicants pay particular attention to potential "disparate impacts" in areas where minorities live in "meaningfully greater" numbers than surrounding regions.

The new rules provoked surprisingly little comment. Many just "saw the guidance as creating yet another section to add to an impact statement" explains Jennifer Hernandez, a San Francisco environmental attorney. In response, companies wanting to build new plants had to start "negotiating with community advocates and federal agencies, offering new computers, job training, school or library improvements, and the like" to grease their projects through.

In December 1997, the Third Circuit Court of Appeals handed the EPA a breathtaking legal victory. It overturned a lower court decision against a group of activists who sued the state of Pennsylvania for granting industrial permits in a town called Chester, and in doing so the appeals court affirmed the EPA'S extension of Civil Rights Act enforcement mechanisms to environmental issues.

(When Pennsylvania later appealed, and the Supreme Court agreed to hear the case, the activists suddenly argued the matter was moot, in order to avoid the Supreme Court's handing down an adverse precedent. This August, the Court agreed, but sent the case back to the Third Circuit with orders to dismiss the ruling. While activists may have dodged a decisive legal bullet, they also wiped from the books the only legal precedent squarely in their favor.)

Two months after the Third Circuit's decision, the EPA issued a second "interim guidance" detailing, for the first time, the formal procedures to be used in environmental justice complaints. To the horror of urban development, business, labor, state, local, and even academic observers, the guidance allows the federal agency to intervene at any time up to six months (subject to extension) after any land-use or environmental permit is issued, modified, or renewed anywhere in the United States. All that's required is a simple allegation that the permit in question was "an act of intentional discrimination or has the effect of discriminating on the basis of race, creed, or national origin."

The EPA will investigate such claims by considering "multiple, cumulative, and synergistic risks." In other words, an individual or company might not itself be in violation, but if, combined with previous (also legal) land-use decisions, the "cumulative impact" on a minority community is "disparate," this could suddenly constitute a federal civil rights offense. The guidance leaves important concepts like "community" and "disparate impact" undefined, leaving them to "case by case" determination. "Mitigations" to appease critics will likewise be negotiated with the EPA case by case.

This "guidance" subjects virtually any state or local land-use decision—made by duly elected or appointed officials scrupulously following validly enacted laws and regulations—to limitless ad hoc federal review, any time there is the barest allegation of racial grievance. Marrying the most capricious elements of wetlands, endangered species, and similar environmental regulations with the interest-group extortion that so profoundly mars urban ethnic politics, the guidance transforms the EPA into the nation's supreme land-use regulator.

Reaction to the Clinton administration's gambit was swift. A coalition of groups usually receptive to federal interventions, including the U.S. Conference of Mayors, the National Association of Counties, and the National Association of Black County Officials, demanded that the EPA withdraw the guidance. The House amended an appropriations bill to cut off environmental justice enforcement until the guidance was revised. This August, EPA officials were grilled in congressional hearings led by Democratic stalwarts like Michigan's John Dingell.

Of greatest concern is the likelihood the guidance will dramatically increase already-crippling regulatory uncertainties in urban areas where ethnic populations predominate. Rather than risk endless delay and EPA-brokered activist shakedowns, businesses will tacitly "redline" minority communities and shift operations to white, politically conservative, less-developed locations.

Stunningly, this possibility doesn't bother the EPA and its environmentalist allies. "I've heard senior agency officials just dismiss the possibility that their policies might adversely affect urban development," says lawyer Hernandez. Dingell, a champion of Michigan's industrial revival, was stunned when Ann Goode, the EPA's civil rights director, said her agency never considered the guidance's adverse economic and social effects. "As director of the Office of Civil Rights" she lectured House lawmakers, "local economic development is not something I can help with."

Perhaps it should be. Since 1980, the economies of America's major urban regions, including Cleveland, Chicago, Milwaukee, Detroit, Pittsburgh, New Orleans, San Francisco, Newark, Los Angeles, New York City, Baltimore, and Philadelphia, grew at only one-third the rate of the overall American economy. As the economies of the nation's older cities slumped, 11 million new jobs were created in whiter areas.

Pushing away good industrial jobs hurts the pocketbook of urban minorities, and, ironically, harms their health in the process. In a 1991 *Health Physics* article, University of Pittsburgh physicist Bernard L. Cohen extensively analyzed mortality data and found that while hazardous waste and air pollution exposure takes from three to 40 days off a life-span, poverty reduces a person's life expectancy by an average of 10 years. Separating minorities from industrial plants is thus not only bad economics, but bad health and welfare policy as well.

Such realities matter little to environmental justice advocates, who are really more interested in radical politics than improving lives. "Most Americans would be horrified if they saw NEJAC [the EPA's environmental justice advisory council] in action," says

Brookings's Foreman, who recalls a council meeting derailed by two Native Americans seeking freedom for an Indian activist incarcerated for killing two FBI officers. "Because the movement's main thrust is toward...`empowerment'..., scientific findings that blunt or conflict with that goal are ignored or ridiculed'"

Yet it's far from clear that the Clinton administration's environmental justice genie can be put back in the bottle. Though the Supreme Court's dismissal of the Chester case eliminated much of the EPA'S legal argument for the new rules, it's likely that more lawsuits and bureaucratic rulemaking will keep the program alive. The success of the environmental justice movement over the last six years shows just how much a handful of ideological, motivated bureaucrats and their activist allies can achieve in contemporary America unfettered by fact, consequence, or accountability, if they've got a President on their side.

11

Environmental Racism Should Be Put in Perspective

Kent Jeffries

Kent Jeffries is with the National Center for Policy Analysis's Washington D.C. office.

Racism is certainly pervasive in American society. But is so-called environmental racism a separate issue, or a mere subset of class and racial privilege? The argument to follow asserts the latter. The author claims that environmental hazards across the board in an advanced nation such as the United States rate comparatively low on the agenda of issues threatening the poor and racially marginalized. Too narrow a focus on environmental racism may distract us from dismantling these oppressive systems of power.

T hose who argue that environmental racism is a serious problem in America, and their numbers are growing, are correct in at least one of their assertions: distinctions based upon race are pervasive in American society. Racism exists. Environmental problems exist. These facts, however, do not reveal whether or not environmental racism has occurred in any given instance. This might be an unimportant distinction but for the fact that some argue that civil rights laws be applied to pollution events and related regulatory violations. Before politicians embark on this course, they should consider the likely impact on the very

"Environmental Racism: A Skeptic's View," Kent Jeffreys, *Journal of Civil Rights and Economic Development*, Spring 1994. Reprinted by permission.

individuals they seek to help. In an era of constrained budgets and sluggish economic expansion, there are precious few resources to divert to low-priority agenda items. The fact remains that even if one-hundred percent of the environmentally "disparate" impact were eliminated, the real problems confronting poor and minority communities would still be unaddressed.

Much of the confusion arises from the fact that most, if not all, disparate environmental impact can be traced to the legacy of prior discrimination in housing, employment, and education. Thus, even the proponents of environmental racism as a new cause of action under civil rights laws are forced to include many non-ecological items within the scope of their complaint.

As one might expect, the topic of environmental racism elicits powerful responses from friend and foe alike. It is unfortunate, however, that the issue is becoming polarized along the traditional conservative-versus-liberal lines of politics. Conservatives abdicate their responsibilities as defenders of individual liberty if they deny even the possibility of the existence of environmental racism, even when it is defined narrowly. Furthermore, for years conservatives fought against federal civil rights laws, often on the basis that "society" was not ready for such changes. This leaves them open to the charge of hiding their bigotry behind an intellectual fig leaf. Too often, the accusation has proved accurate. On the other hand, it appears that much of what makes the issue attractive to liberals is the opportunity to bash industry and conservatives while seeking political gain. That may accurately reflect how the game is played, but it does little to benefit the true victims or to identify the real problems.

I. What Is Environmental Racism?

It was inevitable that someone would associate these two potent political forces.[1] Dr. Benjamin F. Chavis was the first to use the term during protests over the siting of a PCB disposal facility in Warren County, North Carolina, in 1982.[2] More recently, Dr. Chavis (then-executive director of the United Church of Christ Commission for

Racial Justice), in testimony before the U.S. House Committee on the Judiciary's subcommittee on Civil and Constitutional Rights defined environmental racism as:

> racial discrimination in environmental policy making and the unequal enforcement of environmental laws and regulations. It is the deliberate targeting of people of color communities for toxic waste facilities and the official sanctioning of a life threatening presence of poisons and pollutants in people of color communities. It is also manifested in the history of excluding people of color from the leadership of the environmental movement. [3]

At the same hearing Robert D. Bullard, then Professor of Sociology at the University of California at Riverside, defined environmental racism more broadly. In Dr. Bullard's view, "[e]nvironmental racism refers to any policy, practice, or directive that differentially affects or disadvantages (whether intended or unintended) individuals, groups, or communities based on race or color."[4]

There are important distinctions between these two definitions. In the former, Chavis suggests that intent is necessary, while in the latter, Bullard suggests that unintentional results qualify as racism. It is this notion of disparate impact without intent that has created the environmental racism movement. Regardless of whether any particular case fits the definition of environmental racism, the fact remains that environmental problems, from a minority perspective, are rather trivial in most, if not all, environmental inequities.[5]

Taking a global view, the environmental problems which confront the vast majority of people on this planet are not recent (nor even human) in origin. Microbial contamination of water and food remain the primary environmental risks faced by human beings. Yet in America, with isolated exceptions, even poor members of minority groups find most of these worries to be greatly reduced, if not eliminated. The environmental issues most often debated in Congress are largely irrelevant to the average person: global climate change, ozone depletion, acid rain, endangered species, and so on. The animal species dominating inner cities across America—pigeons, rats, and roaches—are hardly endangered. Much has been said of potentially harmful levels of lead in the bloodstream of inner-city minorities. Yet the primary risk of "lead poisoning" in urban areas comes from the mouth of a gun rather than a water faucet or a paint can. Murder is the leading cause of death among young male African Americans. While over 400 people were murdered in Washington, D.C., last year, not a single person died because of groundwater contamination from a hazardous waste site. Environmental issues should be placed in perspective.

II. The Right Site?

Much of the original support for the theory of environmental racism was derived from studies of the siting of hazardous waste facilities. It is difficult to assess hazardous waste facility siting decisions without complete information. However, the definition of "minority community" seems to vary widely in the published reports. In one instance it may refer to a county, in another, a particular neighborhood or postal ZIP code area. It seems that a concerted effort is often made to maximize the apparent racial disparity of hazardous waste siting decisions or pollution events.

As an illustrative example, consider the published reports of the *National Law Journal* ("NLJ"), an organization that has strongly pushed the notion of environmental racism. The *NLJ* reported, as evidence of environmental inequity, that "small fines in minority areas have been lodged against industrial giants: a $22,000 air pollution penalty against Proctor & Gamble Co. in Staten Island, N.Y."[6]

However, Staten Island, overall, is eighty-five percent white. It is also the site of Fresh Kills, the world's largest landfill, which takes in garbage and waste from the other boroughs of New York (which have much higher minority populations). In addition, it is hard to imagine that air pollution on Staten Island can be confined to a particular minority enclave.

Yet in other cases, the *NLJ* cites county population as conclusive evidence of racial discrimination. For example, the infamous PCB disposal facility case[7] in North Carolina arose in "the county with the highest percentage of minority residents in the state."[8] Yet we are not told whether that county also has a low population density, thus providing a nonracial reason to site such a facility. High population densities may be avoided because of a fear of accidents. This would make it more likely that rural sites would be selected. Other considerations that may play a role in site selection include transportation access, existing infrastructure, geophysical conditions, and even climate.

Furthermore, it is often irrelevant (from a human health perspective) how close one is to a site containing potential groundwater contamination. Without knowing the hydrology of an area, it is impossible to predict the flow of the contaminant. Thus, it may actually migrate away from the minority community. Of course, the residents must also rely on the contaminated water source or there will be no human exposure. It would seem likely that the major motivating factor behind such protests is frustration with a political process that permits nuisances (noise, odor, traffic) to move into or near residential neighborhoods or rural communities. Nevertheless, without a consistent standard by which to judge individual cases, "racism" will be in the eye of the beholder. While no empirical study can eliminate the possibility that racism motivated some local decisions, the most thorough national study to date determined that hazardous waste facilities were just as likely to be found in working class white neighborhoods as in any other areas.[9]

Unmentioned through most of this debate is the fact that even the experts on Superfund sites (believed to comprise most of the "worst" waste sites in the country) admit that the health risks from groundwater contamination are low. Undaunted, some have called for an expansion of Superfund to include considerations related to environmental equity.[10] Yet Superfund is an almost complete failure, and racist motivations might be the least of the problems associated with the program. Measured by any reasonable standards, Superfund does not provide significant health or environmental benefits to the American public. Many Superfund sites have required over thirty million dollars in environmental "cleanup" expenditures. Which minority community would not find it more useful to turn at least a portion of such sums toward higher priority expenditures? What if such funds were to some degree available for alternative community investments such as health clinics, scholarship and tutorial funds, public parks, or private police protection? [11] An individual's quality of life is the product of many variables. Focusing on one, in this case the environment, to the exclusion of others may be ineffective or even counterproductive.

In any event, most of the information available on hazardous waste sites does not indicate the actual exposures to potentially hazardous substances. Living next door to a state-of-the-art waste handling facility may expose an individual to less risk than drinking a morning cup of coffee.[12]

III. Low Land Values

Poor people and minorities do not necessarily attract polluters merely because they are poor or people of color or because the polluters are racists. Low-cost land attracts industry for some of the same reasons that it attracts poor people. In many industrial regions, including most of those now condemned as physical evidence of "environmental racism" (the South Side of Chicago, for example) minorities were given their first access to the American Dream. Employers motivated by the capitalistic urge to make a profit, regardless of their personal racism or lack thereof, hired the best workers they could find at the lowest wage they could pay. Regardless of our current attitudes, this often worked to the benefit of the economically disadvantaged especially minorities, giving them their first opportunity to enter the industrial workplace and achieve a decent standard of living. In addition, workers preferred to live close to their place of employment, for obvious reasons. Thus, they moved to the general vicinity of the pollution sources. In fact, this century has witnessed the largest internal migration in American history as rural-born African Americans moved to industrial urban areas. Even with the pollution and the low-wage jobs, their lives were greatly improved. How ironic that the very economic forces that eventually spawned the civil rights movement would be condemned as environmental racism today.

IV. Native American Issues

Environmental racism issues, of course, are not limited to African-American communities. Environmental conditions in Hispanic and Native American communities, among others, are also being examined for evidence of racism. [13]

Admittedly, Native American reservations suffer from enormous problems. However, most of them stem from the welfare state conditions that result from anachronistic federal policies. The reservation system is comprised of apartheid-style homelands, and it suffers from many of the same flaws that its more famous descendant displayed in South Africa. To a large extent, environmental hazards, of the sort typically contemplated by the EPA, are frivolous matters when compared to the very real problems of alcoholism, inadequate health care, inadequate education, inadequate housing, inter alia, that are the rule on reservations. American apartheid is complex: it could not exist without the support of the federal government, which is hopelessly entangled with treaty obligations and patronizing politicians. Moreover, many tribal leaders are willing co-conspirators in the suppression of their kin. Consequently, property rights and individual civil liberties are often ignored or trammelled. These are the results of true racism.

Yet many conclude that hazardous or solid waste siting decisions are always motivated by racism when Native American reservations are involved. Considering that many of the problems confronting reservation residents stem from unemployment, any effort to bring in jobs would at least hold the potential of mitigating the negative effects of the reservation system. The condescending attitude of many well-intentioned individuals, that minorities cannot handle their own affairs, is resultant of the cultural and racial bigotry which permeates this debate.

V. International Examples of Environmental Racism

Of course, racism is not a uniquely American phenomenon. Any examination of current global events would show that race, culture, and religion are the sources of much conflict in the world today. Environmental problems are also universal. Thus, it would be inaccurate to suggest that environmental racism is a purely American phenomenon. In addition, developing countries rarely have sufficient resources or proper political institutions to deal effectively with the environmental agenda of the industrialized nations. Nevertheless, Western standards are often imposed on less developed nations, evoking images of the imperialism of the colonial era. Two of the major issues in this regard are population control and wildlife preservation.

Population Control

Many environmental groups are publicly supportive of population control efforts.[14] Such efforts disproportionately affect people of color around the world, whether intentionally or not. A near constant refrain within the environmental lobby is the claim that the population of the world must be controlled. This demand influences the highest levels of government, as demonstrated by Vice President Albert Gore. In his book, *Earth in the Balance,* Gore outlines five strategic goals necessary "to save the global environment."[15] Gore's first strategic goal is "the stabilizing of world population."[16] Furthermore, the environmental lobby demands that economic growth and aspirations around the world be severely limited, especially in developed nations. However, not all of the scholarly literature supports the assumptions underlying overpopulation concerns.[17] Recently, the African Academy of Sciences rejected international demands for population control measures. According to the official statement: "For Africa, population remains an important resource for development without which the continent's natural resources will remain latent and unexploited.[18]

Wildlife Protection

For years, Richard Leakey, a white man, was Kenya's Director of Wildlife Conservation. Dr. Leakey took his job very seriously; so seriously, in fact, that he created a small, well-armed platoon which was authorized to "shoot to kill" suspected animal poachers. Leakey was a passionate protector of wildlife. He was also a spokesman for Rolex watches. A single Rolex watch costs several times the $400 per capita annual income of black Kenyans. Leakey was also strongly supported by many environmental organizations which do not seem to grasp the antihuman aspects of his stance on wildlife issues. Yet Dr. Leakey's boss, Minister of Tourism and Wildlife Noah Katana Ngala, considered him to be arrogant and racist.[19]

Only in recent years has the general public begun to realize that wildlife should not be cherished above human life. For example, the *New York Times* documented how inappropriate international policies were imposed on native Africans by the environmental lobby.[20] This article exposed the hypocrisy and counterproductive effects of the ban on commerce in ivory. Until the people of Africa are permitted to own the local wildlife, and profit from that ownership, both human rights and wildlife will remain in peril. Two-legged Africans should receive at least the same respect from environmentalists as do four-legged Africans.

VI. Do Environmentalists Hate the Poor?

Such provocative statements are not being made solely by right-wing ideologues seeking politically correct cover. Even avowed socialists have noticed the elitist nature of traditional environmental histories. [21]

The EPA has typically responded to an elite constituency, not minorities or the poor. In most cases, the agenda of the environmental elitists does not coincide with the interests of minorities. As a brief case study, consider the recurrent battle over automobile fuel efficiency. Arguments are sometimes made that higher fuel efficiency would benefit the poor by lowering their cost of transportation. This is simply a political justification seized upon to cover the real impact of these regulations. Higher mileage is strongly correlated with lower vehicle weight. Lower weight unambiguously leads to higher rates of injury and death in car crashes.[22] Recently, a federal circuit court declared that the federal government had distorted and disregarded safety data in an effort to justify higher fuel efficiency standards.[23]

The poor, who are disproportionately comprised of minorities, are even more directly impacted by President Clinton's call for higher gasoline taxes (hidden within his overall BTU Tax Proposal). In his first State of the Union Address, President Clinton claimed higher energy taxes would benefit the environment, among other miraculous results.[24] However, Clinton was forced to admit that gas taxes are punishingly regressive, taking a much bigger bite from the paychecks of the poor than of the rich. Clinton's solution: he cynically proposed to offset the gas tax's impact on the poor by enlarging the federal food stamp program. This is environmental elitism at its worst. Under the guise of an "environmentally important" energy tax, Clinton would take money from the poor and replace it with food stamps. The *Washington Post* reported that Clinton's tax proposal "has the strong support of only one bloc: the environmental lobby."[25] Such environmental policies reduce the independence and well-being of minorities and the poor and compensate them by making them more dependent on the state.

Even if the economic impact of higher energy taxes were quite small, there is an indisputable relationship between human health and human wealth.[26] On average, wealthier is healthier. Around the world, greater prosperity is closely associated with longer life expectancy. Thus, wasting resources in a fruitless search for perfectly safe environments may, in fact, reduce societal well-being. While the United States can afford to spend well over $120 billion on compliance with environmental regulations each year,[27] in developing countries there is no money available for basic health matters, let alone to address minute environmental risks from trace contaminants.

Yet even in America, wasting resources on trivial environmental risks can lower the net wealth of a community, and result in higher mortality rates over time. In other words, environmental regulations should not be based merely on a calculation of costs versus benefits, but rather on risk versus risk.[28] This research should be applied to the question of environmental racism to determine if we are, in fact, overlooking important increases income which more than offset increases in pollution exposure. After all, one of the most unhealthy conditions known to researchers is unemployment. Simply creating jobs in minority communities may correct for any past environmental degradation.

While it can be demonstrated that health improves along with increases in wealth, it appears that personal attitudes also change with economic status. There is much information to suggest that environmental concern rises with prosperity. International studies consistently find that at around $5000 in per capita income, nations begin to stress environmental quality to a relatively higher degree.[29] An American researcher found that the "demand" for environmental quality was similar to the market demand for luxury goods.[30] When the economy grows by a few percent, sales of both BMWs and environmental regulations increase by an even larger percentage.

VII. Cancer Alley

But perhaps the poor and people of color *are* being poisoned by the effluence of our affluent society. Indeed, some have suggested that "people of color are the proverbial canaries in the coal mine"[31] because of inordinate exposure to toxic chemicals. If true, something certainly should be done to protect individuals from what amounts to assault and battery with a deadly chemical. This topic has generated the most passionate arguments from those who detect widespread environmental racism.

Easily the strongest dread generated by environmental concern is the fear of cancer. This is evident in the term coined for the industrial corridor stretching from Baton Rouge to New Orleans, Louisiana, "Cancer Alley."[32] There is no question that the prevalence of petrochemical plants and other industrial activities has strongly impacted the local environment. But was the industrialization motivated by racist impulses? The fact that "Cancer Alley's" hydrocarbon deposits and Mississippi River barge traffic exist independent of skin color or socioeconomic class refute most, but not all, claims of environmental racism in the region. More specific claims of disparate impact and facility siting decisions have been explored by the Louisiana Advisory Committee to the U.S. Commission on Civil Rights.[33] The Committee's report found, unsurprisingly, that conditions in poor, predominantly minority communities were worse than elsewhere. In other words, the Committee found evidence of disparate impact.

However, simply documenting "disparate impact" is not the same as documenting harm, to either individuals or the community at large. All impact is, to a greater or lesser degree, "disparate." To make the case that general environmental exposures in minority communities have measurably harmed individuals, much attention has been granted to cancer and miscarriage rates, especially in Louisiana.

Thus, much of the debate over the existence of community harm has focused on cancer mortality rates, widely considered to be proof of the "Cancer Alley" thesis. It is true that cancer mortality rates in south Louisiana are higher than the national average. Yet this is largely due to the lack of adequate medical care. Therefore, the cancer incidence rate is considered a better indicator of the risk of developing cancer.

For example, one study examined cancer rates in southern Louisiana.[34] "The study found that in contrast to the State's well-documented cancer mortality rates, incidence rates for all cancers combined in south Louisiana are either the same as, or lower than, the national rates."[35] The American Cancer Society's Louisiana division confirmed these findings.[36] Similar results were generated by an examination of purportedly high rates of miscarriages in St. Gabriel, Louisiana.[37] Thus, much of the report focused on non-medical impacts such as nuisance and community disruption or displacement. This begins to shift the complaint onto more familiar territories of property and tort law.

VII. Legal Hurdles

As the statistics seem to indicate, even if environmental racism is practiced in a community, its health effects may be too subtle to detect. This highlights the fact that the primary obstacle to demonstrating the existence of environmental racism is the burden of proof. Most cases have failed to demonstrate racial motivation.[38]

That is the result, quite simply, of its absence. However, that has not prevented some from assuming the primary motivation was racial and that justice was thwarted by exceedingly high judicial standards.[39] Because actual intent to discriminate along racial lines is normally lacking or impossible to document, many commentators have suggested replacing "intent" with "disparate impact."[40]

This is not to suggest, however, that racism does not or cannot exist. In fact, there can be no doubt that racism has been expressed in numerous zoning and siting decisions around the country.[41] However, when it comes to environmental racism, the facts are more confused and the conclusions more ambiguous.[42] Tinkering with the burden of proof or the weight of evidence required in such cases will not change the underlying facts.

Conclusion

Much of what is declared to be environmental racism in America today would be more properly described as elitism. Class privilege and political power are unlikely to be completely eliminated or even satisfactorily dealt with through political action alone. Thus, it would seem that much of the debate over so-called environmental racism is misplaced.

With regard to siting decisions for polluting industries, there should be little doubt that political elites are better situated to influence, even to veto, site selection. Even when elite groups find themselves out-voted, they have a final option often unavailable to poor minorities: they move. Particularly in urban areas, this is how poor and minority neighborhoods are created in the first instance. Migration and demographic shifts will continue to confound simple calculations of institutional racism.

Although racism may permeate society, to date, the examples given have been largely ambiguous and do not make the case that environmental racism is a common variety. Nevertheless, the assumption that civil rights laws will create political and bureaucratic pressures to spend more money on environmental quality in minority communities is probably true, if somewhat exaggerated. Unfortunately, money intended for the poor must run a gauntlet of open palms. This aspect of reality does not change simply because the expenditures are for environmental cleanup rather than food stamps or section 8 housing. Most environmental cleanup money is wasted, just as most welfare program expenditures never make it past the middle class.

The real problem is that America already has over-politicized environmental issues. Since the government now determines how much pollution is appropriate or legally acceptable, the politically powerful, who are best able to focus their attention on state mechanisms of control, will be more likely to have their interests protected.[43] Making environmental racism a political issue will not alter this fact.

However, if the states assume their proper role and explore property rights-based solutions to pollution, a decentralized, self-policing process can arise. Respect for contract and private property will solve much of the apparent dilemma over racially disparate environmental results.

References

1 If one takes an ecological view, it is not surprising that the environmental racism "niche" would eventually be filled by an opportunistic political species.

2 Environmental Racism: Hearings Before the Subcomm on Civil and Constitutional Rights of the House Comm. On the Judiciary, 103d Cong., 1st Sess. (1993) [hereinafter Hearings] (testimony of Dr. Benjamin F. Chavis, Jr., Executive Director of United Church of Christ, Commission for Racial Justice).

3 Id.

4 Hearings, supra note 2 (testimony of Robert D. Bullard).

5 To a certain degree, the expansion of the term "environment" to include all impacts on humans can be socially beneficial. After all, contaminated groundwater is a near-zero risk, while crack cocaine is a high risk to individuals. Thus, so long as priorities are maintained within the total set of "environmental risks," the most significant problems are likely to be dealt with first.

6 Marianne Lavelle, "Negotiations Are Key to Most Fines," *Nat'l L.J.*, Sept. 21, 1992, at S6

7 NAACP v. Gorsuch, No. 82-768 (E.D.N.C. August 10, 1982).

8 Marcia Coyle, "Lawyers Try to Devise New Strategy," *Nat'lL L.J.*, Sept. 21, 1992, at S8.

9 Douglas L. Anderton et al, "Hazardous Waste Facilities: Environmental Equity Issues in Metropolitan Areas," *Evaluation Rev.* April 1994, at 123-40.

10 Among the Superfund issues explored by the National Advisory Council on Environmental Policy and Technology (NACEPT) were environmental justice and nondiscriminatory implementation and enforcement. NACEPT provided its findings to EPA Administrator Carol Browner toward the end of 1993.

11 In fact, it would appear that nonecological amenities and services are the final goal for many within the anti-environmental racism movement. As any political scientist can tell you, public policy surrogates are often utilized to achieve one's true goals. See Lois Swirsky Gold et al., Rodent Carcinogens: Setting Priorities, 258 *Science* 261 (1992). See generally Stephen Breyer, *Breaking the Vicious Circle: Toward Effective Risk Regulation* passim (1993).

13. *See generally* U.S. E.P.A., *Environmental Equity: Reducing Risk for All Communities* passim (1992).

14 Consider the existence of groups such as Zero Population Growth, Negative Population Growth, and the Carrying Capacity Network as well as the population control projects of most major environmental organizations.

15 Albert Gore, *Earth in the Balance* 305 (1992).

16. Id.

See, e.g., David Osterfeld *Prosperity Versus Planning: How government Stifles Economic Growth* (1992); Julian Simon, *Population Matters* (1990); Julian Simon, *The Ultimate Resource* (1981).

18 KS. Jayaraman, "Science Academies Call for Global Goal of Zero Population Growth," *Nature*, Nov. 1993, at 3.

19 See Fiammetta Rocco, "Endangered Species," *Esquire*, April 1994, at 50.

20 Raymond Bonner, "Crying Wolf Over Elephants," *N.Y. Times*, Feb. 7, 1993, at M17. See generally Raymond Bonner, *At the Hand of Man: Peril and Hope for Africa's Wildlife* passim (1993).

21 See Marcy Darnovsky, "Stories Less Told: Histories of U.S. Environmentalism," 92 *Socialist* fu:v. 111, 118 (1992).

22 Robert W. Crandall & John D. Graham, *The Effect of Fuel Economy Standards on Automobile Safety*, 32 J.L. & econ. 97 (1989).

23 Competitive Enter. Inst. V. NHTSA, 956 F.2d 321 (D.C. Cir. 1992).

24 President's Address to Joint Session of Congress on Administrative Goals, 29 Weekly Comp. Pres. Doc. 215 (Feb. 17, 1993).

25 Thomas W. Lippman, "Energy Tax Proposal Has 'Green' Tint," *Wash. Post*, Mar. 2, 1993, at D-1.

26 See Ralph L. Keeney, "Mortality Risks Induced by Economic Expenditures," 10 *Risk Analysis* 147 (1990). Keeney's work served as the basis for Judge Stephen F. Williams' concurring opinion in UAW v. OSHA, 938 F.2d 1310 (D.C. Cir. 1991).

27 Alan Carlin, Environmental Protection Agency, "Environmental Investments: The Cost of a Clean Environment" 2-3 (1990). Carlin calculates 1993 aggregate pollution control costs (in 1986 dollars) as being over $123 billion. Id. Adjusting for inflation would give an approximate figure of $140 billion (in 1993 dollars).

28 See generally Aaron Wildavsky, *Searching for Safety* passim (1988).

29 See generally Gene M. Grossman & Alan B. Kreuger, *Environmental Impacts of a North American Free Trade Agreement* passim (1991).

30 See Don Coursey, *The Demand for Environmental Quality* 14 (1992).

31 Steve Curwood, "Environmental Justice: Continuing the Dialogue, Opening Remarks at the National Conference of the Society of Environmental Journalists," Durham, N.C. (Oct. 22-23, 1993).

32 Conger Beasley, "Of Poverty and Pollution: Keeping Watch in 'Cancer Alley,'" *Buzzworm*, July/Aug. 1990, at 39-45.

33 Louisiana Advisory Comm. to the U.S. Comm. on Civil Rights, *The Battle for Environmental Justice in Louisiana ... Government, Industry, and the People* (1993) [hereinafter *Battle*].

34 See id. At 38 (citing LSU Medical Center in New Orleans's, "Cancer Incidence in South Louisiana," 1983-1986).

35 Id.

36 Id.

37 Id. At 39 (citing Tulane University School of Public Health and Tropical Medicine, "St. Gabriel Miscarriage Investigation East Bank of Iberville Parish, Louisiana (1989).

38 See, e.g., Washington v. Davis, 426 U.S. 229, 246 (1976) (must show intent to discriminate); United States v. Yonkers Bd. Of Educ., 837 F.2d 1181, 1216 (2d Cir. 1987) (impact alone not sufficient, must show intentional discrimination); East Bibb Twiggs Neighborhood Ass'n v. Macon-Bibb Planning & Zoning Comm'n, 706 F. Supp. 880, 886 (M.D. Ga. 1989) (evidence insufficient to establish that land use development motivated by racial dis crimination); Bean v. Southwestern Waste Mgmt. Corp., 482 F. Supp. 673, 677 (S.D. Tex. 1979); .

39 See Rachel D. Godsil, Note, "Remedying Environmental Racism," 90 *Mich. L. Rev.* 394 Passim (1991).

40 See Hearings, supra note 2, at 12 (testimony of Robert D. Bullard).

41 See Clint Bolick, *Grassroots Tyranny: The Limits of Federalism* 169–72 (1993) (describing actions of city government of Yonkers, New York).

42 See Keith Schneider, "Plan for Toxic Dump Pits Blacks Against Blacks," *N.Y. Times*, Dec. 13, 1993, at A12.

43 In the opinion of this author, at least since the Progressive era, government has essentially condemned an easement in favor of pollution across all property (and all people) in America.

12

Corporations and Governments Place Profits Ahead of People

Anup Shah

Anup Shah is the editor of Global Issues, a website whose aim is to raise awareness and provide links to more information for people wanting to look deeper into the issues. Shah resides in the U.K. and has a background in Computer Science.

The West has a history of underdevelopment in Africa. Multinational fossil fuel companies are now going even further, meddling in political affairs and disrupting the peaceful protests of Nigerians concerned about the pillage of their "dark nectar"—the profitable oil that is abundant in the Niger Delta. These oil companies are often in cahoots with military operations that seek to further each other's interests as well. Unfortunately, lack of a free press stifles much of this information from reaching a broader audience.

"There is a symbiotic relationship between the military dictatorship and the multinational companies who grease the palms of those who rule....

They are assassins in foreign lands. They drill and they kill in Nigeria."

—"Assassins in Foreign Lands," A CorpWatch Radio Interview with Human Rights Activist Oronto Douglas

The Niger Delta in Nigeria has been the attention of environmentalists, human rights activists, and fair

"Nigeria and Oil," Anup Shah, Global Issues, June 10, 2010. Reprinted by permission.

trade advocates around the world. The trial and hanging of environmentalist Ken Saro-Wiwa and eight other members of the Ogoni ethnic minority made world-wide attention. So too did the non-violent protests of the Ogoni people. The activities of large oil corporations such as Mobil, Chevron, Shell, Elf, Agip, etc have raised many concerns and criticisms.

A series of repressive and corrupt governments in Nigeria have been supported and maintained by western governments and oil corporations, keen on benefiting from the fossil fuels that can be exploited. As people and transnational oil corporations have been fighting over this "dark nectar" in the delta region, immense poverty and environmental destruction have resulted.

The Ogoni, Ijaw, and other people in the Niger Delta, those who have been worst affected for decades have been trying to stand up for themselves, their environment, and their basic human and economic rights.

The Nigerian government and the oil companies have responded by harshly cracking down on protestors.

Shell, for example, has even been criticized for trying to divide communities by paying off some members to disrupt non-violent protests.

According to Human Rights Watch, "multinational oil companies are complicit in abuses committed by the Nigerian military and police."

An investigation and report by Essential Action and Global Exchange found that:

1. Oil corporations in the Niger Delta seriously threaten the livelihood of neighboring local communities. Due to the many forms of oil-generated environmental pollution evident throughout the region, farming and fishing have become impossible or extremely difficult in oil-affected areas, and even drinking water has become scarce. Malnourishment and disease appear common.

2. The presence of multinational oil companies has had additional adverse effects on the local economy and society,

including loss of property, price inflation, prostitution, and irresponsible fathering by expatriate oil workers.

3. Organized protest and activism by affected communities regularly meet with military repression, sometimes ending in the loss of life. In some cases military forces have been summoned and assisted by oil companies.

4. Reporting on the situation is extremely difficult, due to the existence of physical and legal constraints to free passage and free circulation of information. Similar constraints discourage grassroots activism.

While the story told to consumers of Nigerian crude in the United States and the European Union—via ad campaigns and other public relations efforts—is that oil companies are a positive force in Nigeria, providing much needed economic development resources, the reality that confronted our delegation was quite the opposite. Our delegates observed almost every large multinational oil company operating in the Niger Delta employing inadequate environmental standards, public health standards, human rights standards, and relations with affected communities. These corporations' acts of charity and development are slaps in the face of those they claim to be helping. Far from being a positive force, these oil companies act as a destabilizing force, pitting one community against another, and acting as a catalyst—together with the military with whom they work closely—to some of the violence racking the region today.

—*Oil for Nothing: Multinational Corporations, Environmental Destruction, Death and Impunity in the Niger Delta,* Essential Action and Global Exchange, *January 25, 2000.*

There have been many clear examples of corporate influence in the Nigerian military repressing the protestors. The military have been accused of thousands of killings, house/village burnings, intimidating people, torture, and so on. From Shell's involvement in the killing of Ken Saro-Wiwa to Chevron-marked helicopters carrying Nigerian military that opened fire upon protestors, the corporations are facing harsh criticisms for the way they have been handling (or encouraging) the situation.

Criticisms abound about the way the oil companies have neglected the surrounding environment and health of the local communities. The Niger Delta is the richest area of biodiversity in Nigeria, but regular oil spills that are not cleaned up, blatant dumping of industrial waste and promises of development projects which are not followed through, have all added to the increasing environmental and health problems.

The latest government has tried to be more democratic and open, which provides hope. However, there are still a number of problems to be solved, including corruption and religious tensions between Muslims and Christians. There were riots and killings, for example, at Muslim calls for imposition of Sharia, Islamic criminal law.

Most of the above was written in 2000. Well, into 2004, things have generally not improved. For example, the *International Herald Tribune* reports on a study titled "Peace and Security in the Niger Delta" where amongst other things, the following was noted:

- Shell companies have worsened fighting in the Niger Delta through payments for land use, environmental damage, corruption of company employees, and reliance on Nigerian security forces.
- The action of Shell companies and their staff creates, feeds into, or exacerbates conflict.
- Violence in the Niger Delta kills some 1,000 people each year, on par with conflicts in Chechnya and Colombia
- With over 50 years of presence in Nigeria, it is reasonable to say that the Shell companies in Nigeria have become an integral part of the Niger Delta conflict.

In response to this, Shell had said that they remained "committed to corporate social responsibility, whereas the report was saying that they had not acted that way! Furthermore, Shell made a weak concession and recognized that their development activities in the past "may have been less than perfect." Compare this to the accusation from the report of being part of the conflict for so long and even making things worse, this admission can be regarded as very weak. To the credit of Shell, this December 2003 report was actually commissioned by them. Usually if people are found to be complicit in acts of crime, etc, then some sort of criminal justice is expected. One doesn't expect Shell to have a criminal case of any sort brought against them. The *Tribune* article didn't even raise this as an issue.

Conditions throughout the past few years has not been much better according to Human Rights Watch's 2010 report. They note although free speech and independent media remain robust and there have been some anti-corruption efforts. However, this is overshadowed by religious and inter-communal violence that has seen Muslims and Christians killing each other and by Nigeria's political leaders' "near-total impunity for massive corruption and sponsoring political violence".

Human Rights Watch also summarizes the conditions and situation in the Niger Delta:

> An amnesty for armed militants in the oil-rich Niger Delta led several thousand men, including top militant commanders, to surrender weapons to the government. Since the latest escalation of violence began in early 2006, hundreds of people have been killed in clashes between rival armed groups vying for illicit patronage doled out by corrupt politicians, or between militants and government security forces. Armed gangs have carried out numerous attacks on oil facilities and kidnapped more than 500 oil workers and ordinary Nigerians for ransom during this period. The amnesty offer, announced in June 2009, followed a major military offensive in May against militants in the creeks of Delta State, which left scores dead and thousands of residents displaced.
>
> The government's blanket amnesty, cash payouts to armed militants, and a proposal to give oil-producing communities a 10 percent stake in government oil ventures bought some respite from militant attacks, but further entrenched impunity and failed

to address the government corruption, political sponsorship of violence, and environmental degradation that underlie the violence and discontent in the Niger Delta. A similar amnesty granted to rival armed groups in 2004 failed to end the Niger Delta violence.

—*Nigeria*, World Report 2010, Human Rights Watch

In mid-2010, the US had its own oil scandal; the massive offshore oil spill in the Gulf of Mexico. It has received a lot of media attention because of the enormous environmental and economic damage caused in the region. Although not as big, there have been oil spills in Nigeria too, and as this short news report notes, it has been a long and hard struggle for affected locals to get any notice.

13

India Has Not Done Enough to Protect the Environment After Bhopal

Edward Broughton

Dr. Edward Broughton is the Director or Research and Evaluation for the USAID ASSIST and Health Care Improvement Projects and currently leads a division responsible for more than a dozen studies in eleven countries. He specializes in economic analyses of health programs.

Anyone who lived through the 1980s remembers the Union Carbide disaster in Bhopal, India. It is among the worst industrial accidents in the history of the world. Faulty plant conditions and lax safety standards caused an explosion, and the ensuing toxic plume of gas killed thousands, harming untold more as well. In the aftermath of a protracted legal battle and comparatively small settlement, India has taken some measures to protect the environment while it rapidly grows economically, but still allows pesticide production and other harmful practices to continue.

Abstract

On December 3, 1984, more than 40 tons of methyl isocyanate gas leaked from a pesticide plant in Bhopal, India, immediately killing at least 3,800 people and causing significant morbidity and premature death for many thousands more. The company involved in what became the worst industrial accident in history immediately tried

"The Bhopal Disaster And Its Aftermath: A Review," Edward Broughton, Environmental Health 4 (2005): 6. PMC. Web. October 26, 2016. http://doi.org/10.1186/1476-069X-4-6. Licensed under CC BY 2.0.

to dissociate itself from legal responsibility. Eventually it reached a settlement with the Indian Government through mediation of that country's Supreme Court and accepted moral responsibility. It paid $470 million in compensation, a relatively small amount of based on significant underestimations of the long-term health consequences of exposure and the number of people exposed. The disaster indicated a need for enforceable international standards for environmental safety, preventative strategies to avoid similar accidents, and industrial disaster preparedness.

Since the disaster, India has experienced rapid industrialization. While some positive changes in government policy and behavior of a few industries have taken place, major threats to the environment from rapid and poorly regulated industrial growth remain. Widespread environmental degradation with significant adverse human health consequences continues to occur throughout India.

December 2004 marked the twentieth anniversary of the massive toxic gas leak from Union Carbide Corporation's chemical plant in Bhopal in the state of Madhya Pradesh, India, that killed more than 3,800 people. This review examines the health effects of exposure to the disaster, the legal response, the lessons learned, and whether or not these are put into practice in India in terms of industrial development, environmental management, and public health.

History

In the 1970s, the Indian government initiated policies to encourage foreign companies to invest in local industry. Union Carbide Corporation (UCC) was asked to build a plant for the manufacture of Sevin, a pesticide commonly used throughout Asia. As part of the deal, India's government insisted that a significant percentage of the investment come from local shareholders. The government itself had a 22% stake in the company's subsidiary, Union Carbide India Limited (UCIL) [1]. The company built the plant in Bhopal because of its central location and access to transport infrastructure. The specific site within the city was zoned for light industrial and commercial use, not for hazardous industry. The plant was initially approved only for formulation of pesticides from component chemicals, such as MIC imported from the parent company, in relatively small quantities. However, pressure from competition in the chemical industry led UCIL to implement "backward integration"—the manufacture of raw materials and intermediate products for formulation of the final product within one facility. This was inherently a more sophisticated and hazardous process [2].

In 1984, the plant was manufacturing Sevin at one quarter of its production capacity due to decreased demand for pesticides. Widespread crop failures and famine on the subcontinent in the 1980s led to increased indebtedness and decreased capital for farmers to invest in pesticides. Local managers were directed to close the plant and prepare it for sale in July 1984 due to decreased profitability [3]. When no ready buyer was found, UCIL made plans to dismantle key production units of the facility for shipment to another developing country. In the meantime, the facility continued to operate with safety equipment and procedures far below the standards found in its sister plant in Institute, West Virginia. The local government was aware of safety problems but was reticent to place heavy industrial safety and pollution control burdens on the struggling industry because it feared the economic effects of the loss of such a large employer [3].

At 11.00 PM on December 2, 1984, while most of the one million residents of Bhopal slept, an operator at the plant noticed a small leak of methyl isocyanate (MIC) gas and increasing pressure inside a storage tank. The vent-gas scrubber, a safety device designer to neutralize toxic discharge from the MIC system, had been turned off three weeks prior [3]. Apparently a faulty valve had allowed one ton of water for cleaning internal pipes to mix with forty tons of MIC [1]. A 30 ton refrigeration unit that normally served as a safety component to cool the MIC storage tank had been drained of its coolant for use in another part of the plant [3]. Pressure and heat from the vigorous exothermic reaction in the tank continued to build. The gas flare safety system was out of action and had been for three months. At around 1.00 AM, December 3, loud rumbling reverberated around the plant as a safety valve gave way sending a plume of MIC gas into the early morning air [4]. Within hours, the streets of Bhopal were littered with human corpses and the carcasses of buffaloes, cows, dogs, and birds. An estimated 3,800 people died immediately, mostly in the poor slum colony adjacent to the UCC plant [1,5]. Local hospitals were soon overwhelmed with the injured, a crisis further compounded by a lack of knowledge of exactly what gas was involved and what its effects were [1]. It became one of the worst chemical disasters in history and the name Bhopal became synonymous with industrial catastrophe [5].

Estimates of the number of people killed in the first few days by the plume from the UCC plant run as high as 10,000, with 15,000 to 20,000 premature deaths reportedly occurring in the subsequent two decades [6]. The Indian government reported that more than half a million people were exposed to the gas [7]. Several epidemiological studies conducted soon after the accident showed significant morbidity and increased mortality in the exposed population. These data are likely to under-represent the true extent of adverse health effects because many exposed individuals left Bhopal immediately following the disaster never to return and were therefore lost to follow-up [8].

Aftermath

Immediately after the disaster, UCC began attempts to dissociate itself from responsibility for the gas leak. Its principal tactic was to shift culpability to UCIL, stating the plant was wholly built and operated by the Indian subsidiary. It also fabricated scenarios involving sabotage by previously unknown Sikh extremist groups and disgruntled employees but this theory was impugned by numerous independent sources [1].

The toxic plume had barely cleared when, on December 7, the first multi-billion dollar lawsuit was filed by an American attorney in a U.S. court. This was the beginning of years of legal machinations in which the ethical implications of the tragedy and its affect on Bhopal's people were largely ignored. In March 1985, the Indian government enacted the Bhopal Gas Leak Disaster Act as a way of ensuring that claims arising from the accident would be dealt with speedily and equitably. The Act made the government the sole representative of the victims in legal proceedings both within and outside India. Eventually all cases were taken out of the U.S. legal system under the ruling of the presiding American judge and placed entirely under Indian jurisdiction much to the detriment of the injured parties.

In a settlement mediated by the Indian Supreme Court, UCC accepted moral responsibility and agreed to pay $470 million to the Indian government to be distributed to claimants as a full and final settlement. The figure was partly based on the disputed claim that only 3,000 people died and 102,000 suffered permanent disabilities [9]. Upon announcing this settlement, shares of UCC rose $2 per share or 7% in value [1]. Had compensation in Bhopal been paid at the same rate that asbestosis victims where being awarded in US courts by defendant including UCC—which mined asbestos from 1963 to 1985—the liability would have been greater than the $10 billion the company was worth and insured for in 1984 [10]. By the end of October 2003, according to the Bhopal Gas Tragedy Relief and Rehabilitation Department, compensation had been awarded to 554,895 people for injuries received and 15,310 survivors of those killed. The average amount to families of the dead was $2,200 [9].

At every turn, UCC has attempted to manipulate, obfuscate, and withhold scientific data to the detriment of victims. Even to this date, the company has not stated exactly what was in the toxic cloud that enveloped the city on that December night [8]. When MIC is exposed to 200° heat, it forms degraded MIC that contains the more deadly hydrogen cyanide (HCN). There was clear evidence that the storage tank temperature did reach this level in the disaster. The cherry-red color of blood and viscera of some victims were characteristic of acute cyanide poisoning

[11]. Moreover, many responded well to administration of sodium thiosulfate, an effective therapy for cyanide poisoning but not MIC exposure [11]. UCC initially recommended use of sodium thiosulfate but withdrew the statement later, prompting suggestions that it attempted to cover up evidence of HCN in the gas leak. The presence of HCN was vigorously denied by UCC and was a point of conjecture among researchers [8,11-13].

As further insult, UCC discontinued operation at its Bhopal plant following the disaster but failed to clean up the industrial site completely. The plant continues to leak several toxic chemicals and heavy metals that have found their way into local aquifers. Dangerously contaminated water has now been added to the legacy left by the company for the people of Bhopal [1,14].

Lessons learned

The events in Bhopal revealed that expanding industrialization in developing countries without concurrent evolution in safety regulations could have catastrophic consequences [4]. The disaster demonstrated that seemingly local problems of industrial hazards and toxic contamination are often tied to global market dynamics. UCC's Sevin production plant was built in Madhya Pradesh not to avoid environmental regulations in the U.S. but to exploit the large and growing Indian pesticide market. However the manner in which the project was executed suggests the existence of a double standard for multinational corporations operating in developing countries[1]. Enforceable uniform international operating regulations for hazardous industries would have provided a mechanism for significantly improved in safety in Bhopal. Even without enforcement, international standards could provide norms for measuring performance of individual companies engaged in hazardous activities such as the manufacture of pesticides and other toxic chemicals in India[15]. National governments and international agencies should focus on widely applicable techniques for corporate responsibility and accident prevention as much in the developing world context as in advanced industrial nations[16]. Specifically, prevention should include risk reduction in plant location and design and safety legislation[17].

Local governments clearly cannot allow industrial facilities to be situated within urban areas, regardless of the evolution of land use over time. Industry and government need to bring proper financial support to local communities so they can provide medical and other necessary services to reduce morbidity, mortality, and material loss in the case of industrial accidents.

Public health infrastructure was very weak in Bhopal in 1984. Tap water was available for only a few hours a day and was of very poor quality. With no functioning sewage system, untreated human waste was dumped into two nearby lakes, one a source of drinking water. The city had four major hospitals but there was a shortage of physicians and hospital beds. There was also no mass casualty emergency response system in place in the city[3]. Existing public health infrastructure needs to be taken into account when hazardous industries choose sites for manufacturing plants. Future management of industrial development requires that appropriate resources be devoted to advance planning before any disaster occurs[18]. Communities that do not possess infrastructure and technical expertise to respond adequately to such industrial accidents should not be chosen as sites for hazardous industry.

Since 1984

Following the events of December 3, 1984, environmental awareness and activism in India increased significantly. The Environment Protection Act was passed in 1986, creating the Ministry of Environment and Forests (MoEF) and strengthening India's commitment to the environment. Under the new act, the MoEF was given overall responsibility for administering and enforcing environmental laws and policies. It established the importance of integrating environmental strategies into all industrial development plans for the country. However, despite greater government commitment to protect public health, forests, and wildlife, policies geared to developing the country's economy have taken precedence in the last 20 years[19].

India has undergone tremendous economic growth in the two decades since the Bhopal disaster. Gross domestic product (GDP) per capita has increased from $1,000 in 1984 to $2,900 in 2004 and it continues to grow at a rate of over 8% per year[20]. Rapid industrial development has contributed greatly to economic growth but there has been significant cost in environmental degradation and increased public health risks. Since abatement efforts consume a large portion of India's GDP, MoEF faces an uphill battle as it tries to fulfill its mandate of reducing industrial pollution[19]. Heavy reliance on coal-fired power plants and poor enforcement of vehicle emission laws have resulted from economic concerns taking precedence over environmental protection[19].

With the industrial growth since 1984, there has been an increase in small scale industries (SSIs) that are clustered about major urban areas in India. There are generally less stringent rules for the treatment of waste produced by SSIs due to less waste generation within each individual industry. This has allowed SSIs to dispose of untreated wastewater into drainage systems that flow directly into rivers. New Delhi's Yamuna River is illustrative. Dangerously high levels of heavy metals such as lead, cobalt, cadmium, chrome, nickel, and zinc have been detected in this river, which is a major supply of potable water to India's capital, thus posing a potential health risk to the people living there and areas downstream[21].

Land pollution due to uncontrolled disposal of industrial solid and hazardous waste is also a problem throughout India. With rapid industrialization, the generation of industrial solid and hazardous waste has increased appreciably and the environmental impact is significant[22].

India relaxed its controls on foreign investment in order to accede to WTO rules and thereby attract an increasing flow of capital. In the process, a number of environmental regulations are being rolled back as growing foreign investments continue to roll in. The Indian experience is comparable to that of a number of developing countries that are experiencing the environmental impacts of structural adjustment. Exploitation and export of natural resources has accelerated on the subcontinent. Prohibitions against locating industrial facilities in ecologically sensitive zones have been eliminated while conservation zones are being stripped of their status so that pesticide, cement, and bauxite mines can be built[23]. Heavy reliance on coal-fired power plants and poor enforcement of vehicle emission laws are other consequences of economic concerns taking precedence over environmental protection[19].

In March 2001, residents of Kodaikanal in southern India caught the Anglo-Dutch company Unilever red-handed when they discovered a dumpsite with toxic mercury laced waste from a thermometer factory run by the company's Indian subsidiary, Hindustan Lever. The 7.4 ton stockpile of mercury-laden glass was found in torn stacks spilling onto the ground in a scrap metal yard located near a school. In the fall of 2001, steel from the ruins of the World Trade Center was exported to India apparently without first being tested for contamination from asbestos and heavy metals present in the twin tower debris. Other examples of poor environmental stewardship and economic considerations taking precedence over public health concerns abound[24].

The Bhopal disaster could have changed the nature of the chemical industry and caused a reexamination of the necessity to produce such potentially harmful products in the first place. However the lessons of acute and chronic effects of exposure to pesticides and their precursors in Bhopal has not changed agricultural practice patterns. An estimated 3 million people per year suffer the consequences of pesticide poisoning with most exposure occurring in the agricultural developing world. It is reported to be the cause of at least 22,000 deaths in India each year. In the state of Kerala, significant mortality and morbidity have been reported following exposure to Endosulfan, a toxic pesticide whose use continued for 15 years after the events of Bhopal[25].

Aggressive marketing of asbestos continues in developing countries as a result of restrictions being placed on its use in developed nations due to the well-established link between asbestos products and respiratory diseases. India has become a major consumer, using around 100,000 tons of asbestos per year, 80% of which is imported with Canada being the largest overseas supplier. Mining, production, and use of asbestos in India is very loosely regulated despite the health hazards. Reports have shown morbidity and mortality from asbestos related disease will continue in India without enforcement of a ban or significantly tighter controls [26,27].

UCC has shrunk to one sixth of its size since the Bhopal disaster in an effort to restructure and divest itself. By doing so, the company avoided a hostile takeover, placed a significant portion of UCC's assets out of legal reach of the victims and gave its shareholder and top executives bountiful profits[1]. The company still operates under the ownership of Dow Chemicals and still states on its website that the Bhopal disaster was "caused by deliberate sabotage".[28]

Some positive changes were seen following the Bhopal disaster. The British chemical company, ICI, whose Indian subsidiary manufactured pesticides, increased attention to health, safety, and environmental issues following the events of December 1984. The subsidiary now spends 30–40% of their capital expenditures on environmental-related projects. However, they still do not adhere to standards as strict as their parent company in the UK.[24]

The US chemical giant DuPont learned its lesson of Bhopal in a different way. The company attempted for a decade to export a nylon plant from Richmond, VA, to Goa, India. In its early negotiations with the Indian government, DuPont had sought and won a remarkable clause in its investment agreement that absolved it from all liabilities in case of an accident. But the people of Goa were not willing to acquiesce while an important ecological site was cleared for a heavy polluting industry. After nearly a decade of protesting by Goa's residents, DuPont was forced to scuttle plans there. Chennai was the next proposed site for the plastics plant. The state government there made significantly greater demand on DuPont for concessions on public health and environmental protection. Eventually, these plans were also aborted due to what the company called "financial concerns."

Conclusion

The tragedy of Bhopal continues to be a warning sign at once ignored and heeded. Bhopal and its aftermath were a warning that the path to industrialization, for developing countries in general and India in particular, is fraught with human, environmental, and economic perils. Some moves by the Indian government, including the formation of the MoEF, have served to offer some protection of the public's health from the harmful practices of local and multinational heavy industry and grassroots organizations that have also played a part in opposing rampant development. The Indian economy is growing at a tremendous rate but at significant cost in environmental health and public safety as large and small companies throughout the subcontinent continue to pollute. Far more remains to be done for public health in the context of industrialization to show that the lessons of the countless thousands dead in Bhopal have truly been heeded.

References

1. Fortun K. *Advocacy after Bhopal*. Chicago, University of Chicago Press; 2001. p. 259.
2. Shrivastava P. *Managing Industrial Crisis*. New Delhi, Vision Books; 1987. p. 196.
3. Shrivastava P. *Bhopal: Anatomy of a Crisis*. Cambridge, MA , Ballinger Publishing; 1987. p. 184.
4. Hazardous Installations Directorate. Health and Safety Executive; 2004. Accident Summary, Union Carbide India Ltd., Bhopal, India: December 3, 1984.
5. MacKenzie D. "Fresh evidence on Bhopal disaster." *New Scientist*. 2002; 19
6. Sharma DC. "Bhopal: 20 Years On." *Lancet*. 2005;365:111–112. doi: 10.1016/S0140-6736(05)17722-8.
7. Cassells J. "Sovereign immunity: Law in an unequal world." *Social and legal studies*. 1996;5:431–436.
8. Dhara VR, Dhara R. "The Union Carbide disaster in Bhopal: a review of health effects." *Arch Environ Health*. 2002;57:391–404.
9. Kumar S. "Victims of gas leak in Bhopal seek redress on compensation." *Bmj*. 2004;329:366. doi: 10.1136/bmj.329.7462.366-b.
10. Castleman B PP. Appendix: the Bhopal disaster as a case study in double standards. In: Ives J, editor. *The Export of Hazards: Trans-national Corporations and Environmental Control Issues*. London , Routledge and Kegan Paul; 1985. pp. 213–222.

11. Mangla B. "Long-term effects of methyl isocyanate." *Lancet*. 1989;2:103. doi: 10.1016/S0140-6736(89)90340-1.

12. Varma DR. "Hydrogen cyanide and Bhopal." *Lancet*. 1989;2:567–568. doi: 10.1016/S0140-6736(89)90695-8.

13. Anderson N. "Long-term effects of mthyl isocyanate." *Lancet*. 1989;2:1259. doi: 10.1016/S0140-6736(89)92347-7.

14. Chander J. "Water contamination: a legacy of the union carbide disaster in Bhopal, India." *Int J Occup Environ Health*. 2001;7:72–73.

15. Tyagi YK, Rosencranz A. "Some international law aspects of the Bhopal disaster." *Soc Sci Med*.1988;27:1105–1112. doi: 10.1016/0277-9536(88)90305-X.

16. Carlsten C. "The Bhopal disaster: prevention should have priority now." *Int J Occup Environ Health*. 2003;9:93–94.

17. Bertazzi PA. "Future prevention and handling of environmental accidents." *Scand J Work Environ Health*. 1999;25:580–588.

18. Dhara VR. "What ails the Bhopal disaster investigations? (And is there a cure?)" *Int J Occup Environ Health*. 2002;8:371–379.

19. EIA. In: India: environmental issues. energy D, editor. http://www.eia.doe.gov/emeu/cabs/indiaenv.html

20. CIA *The World Factbook: India*. http://www.cia.gov/cia/publications/factbook/geos/in.html#Econ.

21. Rawat M, Moturi MC, Subramanian V. "Inventory compilation and distribution of heavy metals in wastewater from small-scale industrial areas of Delhi, India." *J Environ Monit*. 2003;5:906–912. doi: 10.1039/b306628b.

22. Vijay R, Sihorwala TA. Identification and leaching characteristics of sludge generated from metal pickling and electroplating industries by Toxicity Characteristics Leaching Procedure (TCLP)Environ Monit Assess. 2003;84:193–202. doi: 10.1023/A:1023363423345.

23. Karliner J. *The Corporate Planet*. San Francisco, Sierra Club Books; 1997. p. 247.

24. Bruno KKJ. *Earthsummit.biz:The Corporate Takeover of Sustainable Development*. Oakland, Ca: First Food Books; 2002. p. 237.

25. Power M. "The poison stream: letter from Kerala." *Harper's*. 2004;August, 2004:51–61.

26. Joshi TK, Gupta RK. "Asbestos in developing countries: magnitude of risk and its practical implications." *Int J Occup Med Environ Health*. 2004;17:179–185.

27. Joshi TK, Gupta RK. "Asbestos-related morbidity in India." *Int J Occup Environ Health*. 2003;9:249–253.

28. Union Carbide Bhopal Information Center. wwwbhopalcom/ucshtm. 2005.

29. Corporate Watch UK. "DuPont: A corporate profile." http://www.corporatewatch.org.uk/profiles/dupont/dupont4.htm.

30. Beckett WS. "Persistent respiratory effects in survivors of the Bhopal disaster." *Thorax*. 1998;53 Suppl 2:S43–6.

31. Misra UK, Kalita J. "A study of cognitive functions in methyl-iso-cyanate victims one year after bhopal accident." *Neurotoxicology*. 1997;18:381–386.

32. Irani SF, Mahashur AA. "A survey of Bhopal children affected by methyl isocyanate gas." *J Postgrad Med*. 1986;32:195–198.

14

Environmentalism Must Bridge Its Racial Divide

Brentin Mock

Brentin Mock is a staff writer at CityLab. He was previously the justice editor at Grist.

The average person of color is just as concerned about environmental degradation, pollution, and climate change as the next person. Yet, all too often people of color are systematically excluded from employment and a voice within mainstream environmental groups. While leaders of NGOs such as Greenpeace have time and again failed to examine their own biases, this has to change, and there is evidence it is— slowly. The history of environmentalism is marked by tensions with other struggles for social justice, but if an environmental movement is to matter, it must be more than a reflection of white values.

This story was originally published on Grist.

> *Out of the rack and ruin of our gangster death,*
> *The rape and rot of graft, and stealth, and lies,*
> *We, the people, must redeem*
> *The land, the mines, the plants, the rivers*
> *The mountains and the endless plain –*
> *All, all the stretch of these great green states –*
> *And make America again!*
>
> – Langston Hughes, 1938

"Are There Two Different Versions of Environmentalism, One 'White,' One 'Black'?" Brentin Mock, *Mother Jones*, July 31, 2014.Reprinted by permission.

I really didn't want to have to address this. While reading through University of Michigan professor Dorceta Taylor's latest report, "The State of Diversity in Environmental Organizations," and thinking about what I would write about it, I had hoped to focus on the solutions. Those solutions—confronting unconscious and subconscious bias and other subtle forms of discrimination—are the parts I had hoped environmentalists would be eager to unpack.

I thought they'd read about the "green ceiling," where mainstream green NGOs have failed to create a workforce where even two out of 10 of their staffers are people of color, and ask themselves what could they do differently. I thought, naively, that this vast report, complete with reams of data and information on the diversity problem, would actually stir some environmentalists to challenge some of their own assumptions about their black and brown fellow citizens.

I was wrong.

Maybe I'm being too harsh. Some green leaders have taken this issue to heart. Frances Beinecke, president of the Natural Resources Defense Council, said in response to the report that the "environmental community has to do more," and that, "Without collective action to create inclusive workplaces, broaden our community partnerships, and diversify our voice, we will not be equipped to confront the great environmental problems of our time."

Michael Brune, executive director of the Sierra Club, responded that his group (which helped fund the report) is "working hard to ensure our organization looks like America."

And yet, judging from the comments on my first story about the report—some from people who profess to spending years and even decades in the green movement—it appears that too many would rather accommodate their prejudices than test their understanding of how non-white, non-hetero, non-male, non-college-educated, non-wealthy human beings relate to the environment.

Worse, too many believe that those in these "non-" categories don't have the skills or knowledge to be valuable to the environmental activism workforce. Too many believe the poor are too occupied with being poor, or black people are too occupied with being black to be occupied in green organizations.

Taylor's report paints a different picture: "A significant number of talented ethnic minorities are willing and able to work in environmental organizations, but discriminatory hiring practices prevent them from obtaining jobs in such organizations."

Her research not only proves this, but her MELDI website also does some of the work for employers, by listing hundreds of professionals of color with bona fide environmental pedigrees.

This week, a group of prominent environmental leaders of color also launched the Diverse Environmental Leaders National Speakers Bureau to draw attention to even more people of color working in the environmental field. If that wasn't enough, Green for All also released results of a survey showing majorities in communities of color support action on climate change and environmental matters.

"There is a lot of rumor and speculation surrounding what people of color think about climate change and the environment," Green For All Executive Director Nikki Silvestri said in a press statement this week. "People of color care deeply about the environment and the impacts of climate change. We understand the urgency of these threats because we experience the effects every single day."

Protecting the environment we live in is not a novel concept for us. Consider the 1960s Harlem survey referenced in Taylor's report, where residents were asked what they liked least about their neighborhoods. The top response from black Harlem was not low wages or police brutality; it was that they did not have enough trees and plants.

The conservationist Charles E. Little, who taught environmentalists most of what they know about "greenways" and green spaces, had a good sense of this. He was an early critic of those who drew "erroneous conclusions" and "simplistic assessments" about what people of color think of the environment. Taylor references his work, also.

Little was responding to studies in the 1960s where researchers argued that black and brown people's own cultures held them back from being more active participants in what are traditionally recognized as environmental causes. It's a tired argument used often as a convenient, if not lazy, way of hiking around the rockier points of racism and discrimination. It's also a convenient way to filter people of color out of a job applicant pool.

***

One reason green groups have been suboptimal in connecting with people of color—and getting them on the payroll—may be that they are speaking a different language when it comes to the environment.

Check the history: In the wake of the 1968 assassination of Martin Luther King, civil rights activism was waning. Meanwhile, momentum was growing around ecological activism, with a lot of hype around organizing for Earth Day. Many African Americans were concerned that funds and resources needed for civil rights reforms were being diverted to new environmental causes. People of color didn't necessarily oppose environmental activism; they just didn't want it to come at the expense of civil and human rights.

Also, the environmental conversation at the time was obsessed with two things: pollution and population. On pollution, it appeared white people were more concerned with cleaning up and preserving uninhabited lands—or what was perceived as uninhabited—to expand parks and wilderness areas.

As noted in Taylor's report:

> Native Americans … disrupted Earth Day proceedings in 1970 to challenge the policymaking process by White environmentalists that left tribes out of decision-making processes related to Indian affairs. Gaylord Nelson, one of the sponsors and key supporters of the event, was greeted by Indian demonstrators who threw garbage on the stage and accused him of sponsoring legislation

that would take land away from the Chippewa tribe to facilitate the creation of a national park.

And then there was the overpopulation alarm that drove many white people into the new environmentalism. The theory, made popular in 1968 by Paul and Anne Ehrlich's book *The Population Bomb*, was that as population increases so does overconsumption and other human activities that wreak havoc on climate and habitat. People of color sensed—right or wrong—a more nefarious agenda here, though.

First, there were the political implications of population—with booming black and brown populations comes increased voting power. Since the 1965 Voting Rights Act prevented discrimination at the polls, their population increases could translate for many whites as a recipe for their loss of control over the government. Once you added in the history of sterilization experiments —like the eugenics project practiced on African Americans in North Carolina, which the state is paying reparations for today—black and brown Americans could not be blamed for thinking there was a racist element to this new environmentalism.

Ironically, black people in the 1960s were as concerned about overpopulation as their white eco-counterparts. After all, it was black and Latino Americans who were mostly living in overcrowded ghettos at the time, and dying from the pollution and disease that came with that. White environmentalists and population zealots, meanwhile, gave off the impression that it was the black and brown population itself that was the pollution problem—an idea that had existed since the beginning of nature conservation in America. If you don't believe me, see Madison Grant.

The 1969 Rockefeller Report on Population Growth and the American Future dispelled many of these notions, stating, "the idea that our population growth is primarily fueled by the poor and the minorities having lots of babies is a myth."

The responses the Rockefeller Commission collected in its own surveys on the topic were telling. Dr. Eugene S. Callender, president of the New York Urban Coalition, told the commission:

Minority groups must share the generally growing concern for the quality of life available to us as the population increases. However, it must also be kept in mind that minority groups have only recently been allowed to become participants in this system, to receive its benefits and to share in shaping its future. We are even more anxious about our position within the society, since our few gains are, even now, tenuous.

Another respondent said, "If this [ecology] movement also talks about fewer people, the question of 'who gets to survive' is raised. So, to us, it becomes 'every man for himself' now, because we have no reason to expect that we won't get the worst of this one too."

It was clear at this point that "environment" meant something different to people of different races. In the 1970 article "Black Ecology," by Nathan Hare, who developed the first collegiate black studies program, he wrote:

The legitimacy of the concept of black ecology accrues from the fact that: (1) the black and white environments not only differ in degree but in nature as well; (2) the causes and solutions to ecological problems are fundamentally different in the suburbs and ghetto (both of which human ecologists regard as "natural [or ecological] areas"; and (3) the solutions set forth for the "ecological crisis" are reformist and evasive of the social and political revolution which black environmental correction demands.

Terry Jones took it a step further calling it "Apartheid Ecology" in the May 1975 edition of *Black World*:

[T]he popularization of the concept of ecology in everyday American life is potentially one of the most relevant forces imaginable in the ultimate liberation of Black America, and it has become such a force in spite (or perhaps because) of the fact that it blatantly overlooks Black Americans and their environmental interests.

While Hare and Jones were attempting to carve out a new definition of environmentalism that spoke more directly to black people's lives, it turns out they may have been closer to the term's true meaning to begin with. As Hare explained in his article, "[T]he word 'ecology' was derived by a German biologist from the word 'aikos' meaning 'house.'"

This more urbanized rendering of the term is not some relic of the "Black Power" era. California State University professor Stephan Mexal, whom I talked to for this story on the Central Park Five, wrote in the 2004 book, *Eco-man: New Perspectives on Masculinity and Nature*:

> The recent spate of critical attention paid to environmental concerns has—perhaps unsurprisingly—tended to assume a rather narrow conception of what, exactly, constitutes the environmental. In its popular usage (for example, 'trying to save the environment'), the term becomes roughly equivalent to natural or is simply used to signify the out-of-doors, the organic. But its etymological roots lie in the Anglo-French *environner* (loosely, to physically encircle), and as such it is crucial to reconnect our awareness of both the environmental and the ecological to a sociologically based understanding of proximate space. Proximate space is our immediate, familiar environment: not, for most Americans, a space of trees and streams and hills but rather a space of concrete and glass and steel.

***

So, historically there's been somewhat of a language barrier between the races in the environmental movement. We define nature by what we see when we look outside. What a black child from Southside Chicago sees through her glass will be different than what a white child sees from her window in South Burlington, Vt.

But regardless of the lens and definitions, there are common understandings and goals across racial and social spectrums. The main commonality is the concern for future generations, which Taylor has pointed out in some her early research.

"It's not necessarily that there is a 'black ecology' and 'white ecology,'" Taylor said in an interview this week. "It's just that our lived experiences with environment are different. White people bring their experience to the discussion— that's why they focus on the birds, trees, plants, and animals, because they don't have the experience of being barred from parks and beaches. It's just a different frame. But overall, we want the same thing: safe places to live, work and play, clean spaces and sustainable, long-lasting communities."

This was acknowledged in the 2005 report "The Soul of Environmentalism," an environmental justice response to the doomsday report "The Death of Environmentalism," which downplayed if not ignored the activism of people of color. The "Soul" report made many of the same points Taylor made in her most recent diversity study:

> The mainstream environmental movement has been unable to racially integrate its senior staff, not because of overt discrimination but because of differences in vision. Many environmentalists of color admire the mainstream movement's goals, but they also know firsthand that social justice is routinely ignored in the mainstream movement's decision-making.

Similar points were made in the environmental justice movement's 1990 letter to mainstream green groups, and also in the seminal "Toxic Waste and Race" report of 1987 that helped spur the movement into its own action. And yet some white environmentalists continued to believe that black and brown Americans' absence among the environmental activism was due to their own lack of agency.

Again, Taylor doin' the knowledge on this:

> Research of this nature continued into the new millennia as scholars and environmental activists often depict ethnic minorities as disinterested in the environment and ignorant of environmental affairs. **These studies also enshrined the idea that minorities were neither qualified for environmental jobs nor wanted such jobs** (Taylor 2000a, 2007; 2008). This logic partly explains why racial diversity has been such a low priority for environmental organizations. **If minorities are not interested in the environment, lack knowledge of it, are**

not qualified, and do not want to work in environmental organizations, why recruit and hire them? [Emphasis added.]

This is why it is so difficult to focus on solutions to the diversity problem—because too many are stuck on racial attitudes popularized when the Klan was chasing sweaty, bulging-eye, watermelon-devouring black sharecroppers through Jim Crow forests, as in the 1915 film *Birth of a Nation*. In that film, screened at the White House to President Woodrow Wilson's applause, black people were seen as something separate from the vision of nature carried by many powerful white conservationists—President Wilson among them.

Black people were seen as crimes against this particular vision of nature, as were Native Americans before them. Since they could no longer be tamed and domesticated as slaves, they needed to be erased.

We've struggled for visibility and recognition among environmentalists ever since. When we created our environmental movement, it was ignored and underfunded. Why? Perhaps because too many white men have built a definition of "environment" that they've determined to be the only truth—a truth that for the rest of us, they believe, is simply not in our nature.

15

"Big Green" NGOs Placate Liberal Consciences, but Do Little Good

Kat Stevens

As a cultural creator, Kat Stevens designs and facilitates original workshops and presentations addressing and connecting issues such as environmental racism, settler colonialism, food justice, prison abolition, and mass incarceration.

The so-called "big green" NGOs, high-profile environmental groups that many people associate with the movement for justice, may not be true allies to people of color and others seeking redress of environmental racism and injustice. In fact, these venerable institutions may render would-be activists ineffectual, convincing them that donating money or divestment campaigns are their best means of action. These status-quo friendly practices discourage, and possibly even dismantle, the movement for more transformative thought and action.

We are living in an age of world-wide energy and financial crises. In Westernized nations like the one I live in, poor rural communities are suffering now: small Appalachian communities ravaged by mountain-top removal mining, rural farms surrounded by frack wells. But what about the communities we don't hear about?

"Are Mainstream Environmental Groups Keeping Racism Alive?" Kat Stevens, *Policy.Mic*, July 26, 2013. Reprinted by permission.

Here we need look no further than Houston's toxic East End, a textbook example of environmental racism, where mostly Latina/o children living fence-line to industry are poisoned mercilessly by refineries like Shell, Exxon, and Valero. Environmental racism (ER) is just another form of systemic racism, the ongoing legacy of colonialism, genocide, and slavery. ER is the intentional and systematic targeting of communities of color with respect to environmental hazards and failure to enforce environmental regulations. For businesses which threaten public and environmental health, it is easier to operate near low-income communities of color with less political and economic power to resist.

When we remove the American-centric lens we are encouraged to view the world through, we see that environmental racism is a global phenomenon. Because of globalization, an ambiguous term that is usually laden with warm connotations of unification, corporations are highly mobile. This makes it easy to travel anywhere in the world to maximize profits through the least government and environmental regulations, the best tax incentives, and the cheapest labor (easily exploitable communities). Consequently, we see the destruction of indigenous cultures, livelihoods, and the fragile and unique ecosystems that plant, animal, and human life alike depend upon to sustain.

Some Americans who consider themselves "well-meaning," "left-leaning," "liberal," "earth-friendly," etc. recognize the corruption and get sad, upset, and restless. If not pacified, they could become a threat to the status quo.

Enter the most powerful tool of the environmental movement: the big green non-governmental organization (NGO).

Big green NGOs present an exciting semblance of resistance that tells Americans that they can make a difference just by clicking here, signing there, sending in monthly donations, watching a flashy video about an adventurous "direct action" that cost hundreds of thousands of dollars to pull off, and making bi-annual trips to the White House to really give that darn president a piece of your mind!

These "movements" seem to do everything in their power to placate, pacify, and render ineffective their target consumers: white, liberal Americans with a small sense of the hollowness of everyday life in capitalist America. By proposing simple and false solutions inside a framework of "peaceful resistance," potential disruptors of the status quo are rendered ineffective while believing they are engaged in meaningful resistance.

In reality, the mainstream environmental movement in the U.S. has done almost nothing to counter the political and economic conditions that make participation in environmental movements an impossibility for many people from the very low-income communities of color that are bearing the brunt of the assault.

Tom Goldtooth, the Executive Director of the Indigenous Environmental Network, said in a 2011 interview with *Africa Report*, "If you look at the NGOs, these are European 'white' NGOs, and there is tremendous racism and classism woven into that. When an ethnic person speaks up, they get offended they don't want a solution from the marginalized. They want to devise the solution they feel is best for the whole system—and we have to ask ourselves what the system they actually represent, entails ... We challenged the big organizations with environmental racism including Greenpeace and Sierra Club, to bring our voices to the board ... They resisted us.

"Look at 350.org—we had to challenge them to bring us to stand with them on the pipeline issue. Bill McKibben, the Ivory Tower white academic, didn't even want to take the time to bring people of color to the organizing."

350.org, just one example of a problematic NGO, has the look and feel of an authentic grassroots movement, but in reality it is a multi-million dollar campaign outfitted with a staff that receives six-figure checks. In addition to placating the public and perpetuating systemic racism, 350.org has received funding from the Rockefeller family, one of the most elite and nefarious families of all time.

Their most insidious superficial means of appeasement? Promoting divestment campaigns, an easy way to quell would-be radicals on college campuses by exploiting impressionable students to spend vast amounts of time, energy, and resources to divest their schools from fossil fuels, which are arguably not only a waste of time, but overtly counterproductive.

We must refuse to be obedient and passive "movement builders" armed with e-mail lists, invoking the name of Bill McKibben, and marching towards the next carefully calculated, police-approved, staged "action." The stakes are so high, with 400,000 people, mostly people of color, dying each year from climate-related disasters. Time is running out for countering the damage that has been done to the global environment. We must dismantle not only capitalism and globalization, but the mainstream NGO trope along with them.

Organizations to Contact

The editors have compiled the following list of organizations concerned with the issues debated in this book. The descriptions are derived from materials provided by the organizations. All have publications or information available for interested readers. The list was compiled on the date of publication of the present volume; the information provided here may change. Be aware that many organizations take several weeks or longer to respond to inquiries, so allow as much time as possible.

EarthAction
PO Box 63 Amherst, MA 01004
Email: contact@earthaction.org
Website: www.earthaction.org

EarthAction's mission is to inform and inspire people everywhere to turn their concern, passion, and outrage into meaningful action for a more just, peaceful, and sustainable world. The organization has spearheaded campaigns to ban the burning of PVC plastics, rid the world of nuclear weapons, and support the advancement of renewable energy.

EarthJustice
50 California Street, Suite 500 San Francisco, CA 94111
(800) 584-6460
Website: www.earthjustice.org

EarthJustice is the largest and oldest nonprofit environmental law organization in the United States. EarthJustice has fought for the country's wildlife and nature preserves, clean energy, a healthy climate, and healthier communities for everyone. Additionally, EarthJustice features an international program that addresses human rights, trade, and environmental issues; a communications team to build a groundswell of public support for the issues and cases we take on; and a policy and legislative team to craft laws that support and extend our gains and to prevent legislative efforts that undermine environmental progress.

Energy Justice Network
1434 Elbridge St. Philadelphia, PA 19149
(215) 743-4884
Website: www.energyjustice.net

Energy Justice Network aims to empower the grassroots through various tools, including community organizing support and advice, student organizing, network-building, research on corporations, policies and technologies, limited legal and technical guidance, and its mapping project. Energy Justice Network understands that energy issues have profound impacts on many other environmental issues from agriculture to waste and recognizes that low-income communities and communities of color tend to be the most seriously impacted by polluting energy systems.

Environmental Health Coalition
2727 Hoover Ave. Suite 202 National City, CA 91950
(619) 474-0220
Website: www.environmentalhealth.org/index.php/en/who-we
-are/mission/environmental-justice

Environmental Health Coalition fights against environmental racism, which is defined as: policies and activities of governments, corporations, educational institutions, or other large organizations with the power to influence many people that, either intentionally or unintentionally, result in people of color and/or low-income people being exposed to greater environmental hazards.

Environmental Justice Clinic
1311 Miller Drive, Room G287 Coral Gables, FL 33146-8087
(305) 284-3934
Website: www.law.miami.edu/academics/center-for-ethics-and
-public-service/environmental-justice-project

As part of the University of Miami School of Law, the Environmental Justice Clinic provides rights education, interdisciplinary research, and public policy resources to low- and moderate-income communities seeking fair treatment and meaningful involvement in the development, implementation, and enforcement of environmental laws, regulations, and policies, including incinerator contamination and industrial pollution.

Natural Resources Defense Council (NDRC)

40 West 20th Street, 11th Floor New York, NY 10011
(212) 727-2700
Website: www.nrdc.org/about

NRDC works to safeguard the earth—its people, its plants and animals, and the natural systems on which all life depends. NRDC combines the power of more than two million members and online activists with the expertise of some 500 scientists, lawyers, and policy advocates across the globe to ensure the rights of all people to the air, the water, and the wild.

Power Shift Network

1752 Columbia Ave. Washington, DC 20009
(202) 299-9072
Website: www.powershift.org

The Power Shift Network is committed to investing in a grassroots, bottom-up movement of young people to mitigate climate change and create a just, clean energy future and resilient, thriving communities for all. The Power Shift Network believes in the need to dismantle the systems of oppression that assign unearned privileges based on race, class, and gender and to provide solutions to energy problems that everyone can participate in and everyone can benefit from.

Sierra Club
2101 Webster St. Suite 1300 Oakland, CA 94612
(415) 977-5500
Website: www.sierraclub.org/environmental-justice

The nation's largest and most influential grassroots environmental organization, the Sierra Club works diligently to explore the integration of social justice and environmental concerns. Its environmental justice program seeks to provide an effective framework for addressing the damage, risk, and discrimination that faces many communities today. By encouraging, connecting, and advising grassroots and community organizations, we hope to foster the growth of the environmental justice movement so that oppressed communities will find justice and everyone can experience the benefits of a healthy and sustainable future.

US Environmental Protection Agency (EPA)
1200 Pennsylvania Avenue, NW Washington, DC 20460
(202) 272-0167
Website: www.epa.gov

The mission of the EPA is to protect human health and the environment. The EPA is strongly committed to environmental justice. Its goal is for all communities throughout the United States to enjoy the same degree of protection from environmental health hazards as well as equal access to the decision-making process to have a healthy environment in which to live, learn, and work.

Bibliography

Books

Rhuks Temitope Ako. *Environmental Justice in Developing Countries: Perspectives from Africa and Asia-Pacific.* Abingdon, Oxon: Routledge, 2013.

Elizabeth Ammons and Modhumita Roy. *Sharing the Earth: An International Environmental Justice Reader.* Athens, GA: University of Georgia Press, 2015.

Robert D. Bullard. *Confronting Environmental Racism: Voices from the Grassroots.* Chicago, IL: South End Press, 1993.

Robert D. Bullard. *Dumping in Dixie: Race, Class, and Environmental Quality.* Boulder, CO: Westview Press, 2000.

Melissa Checker. *Polluted Promises: Environmental Racism and the Search for Justice in a Southern Town.* New York, NY: 2005.

Joseph R. DesJardins. *Environmental Ethics: An Introduction to Environmental Philosophy.* Boston, MA: Wadsworth Cengage Learning, 2013.

Trevor K. Fuller. *Environmental Justice and Activism in Indianapolis.* Lanham, MD: Lexington Books, 2015.

Barry E. Hill. *Environmental Justice: Legal Theory and Practice.* Washington, DC: ELI Press, 2012.

David M. Konisky. *Failed Promises: Evaluating the Federal Government's Response to Environmental Justice.* Cambridge, MA: The MIT Press.

Stephanie A. Malin. *The Price of Nuclear Power: Uranium Communities and Environmental Justice.* New Brunswick, NJ: Rutgers University Press, 2015.

Michael Mascarenhas. *Where the Waters Divide: Neoliberalism, White Privilege, and Environmental Racism in Canada.* Lanham, MD: Lexington Books, 2012.

Christina Robertson and Jennifer Westerman. *Working on Earth: Class and Environmental Justice.* Reno, NV: University of Nevada Press, 2015.

Dorceta E. Taylor. *Toxic Communities: Environmental Racism, Industrial Pollution, and Residential Mobility.* New York, NY: NYU Press, 2014.

Gordon P. Walker. *Environmental Justice.* New York, NY: Routledge, 2012.

Carl A. Zimring. *Clean and White: A History of Environmental Racism in the United States.* New York: New York University Press, 2015.

Periodicals and Internet Sources

Cara Bayles. "Behind Bars on Polluted Land," *The Atlantic*, May 24, 2016. http://www.theatlantic.com/health/archive/2016/05/behind-bars-on-polluted-land/484202/.

Laura Bradley. "E-Waste in Developing Countries Endangers Environment, Locals," US News.com, August 1, 2014. http://www.usnews.com/news/articles/2014/08/01/e-waste-in-developing-countries-endangers-environment-locals.

Julie Cart. "A Strong Voice in Louisiana's Cancer Alley," *Los Angeles Times*, August 27, 2013. http://www.latimes.com/local/great-reads/la-me-c1-subra-enviro-20130827-dto-htmlstory.html.

Rachel Cernansky. "Cancer Alley: Big Industry and Bigger Illness Along Mississippi River," treehugger.com, February 8, 2011. http://www.treehugger.com/corporate-responsibility/cancer-alley-big-industry-bigger-illness-along-mississippi-river.html.

Nick Chiles. "8 Horrifying Examples of Corporations Mistreating Black Communities with Environmental Racism," Atlanta Black Star," February 12, 2015. http://atlantablackstar.com/2015/02/12/8-horrifying-examples-of-corporations-mistreating-black-communities-with-environmental-racism.

The Economist. "In Whose Backyard?" *The Economist,* December 2, 2010. http://www.economist.com/node/17633240.

John Eligon. "A Question of Environmental Racism in Flint," *The New York Times*, January 21, 2016. http://www.nytimes.com/2016/01/22/us/a-question-of-environmental-racism-in-flint.html.

Charles D. Ellison. "Racism in the Air You Breathe: When Where You Live Determines How Fast You Die," The Root, August 17, 2015. http://www.theroot.com/articles/culture/2015/08

/environmental_racism_when_where_you_live_determines
_how_fast_you_die.

David J. Krajicek. "Flint Is Part of a Pattern: 7 Toxic Assaults on Communities of Color," Salon, January 26, 2016. http://www .salon.com/2016/01/26/the_hideous_racial_politics_of _pollution_partner.

Kristen Lombardi. "Environmental Racism Persists amid EPA Inaction," MSNBC, August 3, 2015. http://www.msnbc.com /msnbc/environmental-racism-persists-amid-epa-inaction.

Brian Mackay. "Hazardous Waste Dumping in Developing Countries," Sustainability and Environmental Justice," October 13, 2014. http://sustainabilityjjay.org/2014/10/hazardous-waste -dumping-in-developing-countries.

James North. "Ecuador's Battle for Environmental Justice Against Chevron," *The Nation*, June 2, 2015. https://www.thenation.com /article/ecuadors-battle-environmental-justice-against-chevron. Minnie Bruce Pratt. "Alabama Community Fights Environmental Racism," Workers World, April 6, 2016. http:// www.workers.org/2016/04/06/alabama-community-fights-environmental-racism/#.V-WThJMrKis.

John Vidal. "Toxic 'e-waste' Dumped in Poor Nations, Says United Nations," *The Guardian*, December 14, 2013. https://www .theguardian.com/global-development/2013/dec/14/toxic -ewaste-illegal-dumping-developing-countries.

Sadhbh Walshe. "'Environmental Racism': Bronx Activists Decry Fresh Direct's Impact on Air Quality," *The Guardian*, March 9, 2015. https://www.theguardian.com/us-news/2015/mar/09/fresh -direct-south-bronx-clean-air-environmental-racism.

Brandi M. White and Eric S. Hall. "Perceptions of Environmental Health Risks Among Residents in the "Toxic Doughnut:" Opportunities for Risk Screening and Community Mobilization," Biomed Central Public Health, December 10, 2015. http://www .ncbi.nlm.nih.gov/pmc/articles/PMC4676177.

Index